EXERCISES IN
VISUAL THINKING

Exercises in
VISUAL
THINKING

by Ralph E. Wileman

VISUAL COMMUNICATION BOOKS

Hastings House, Publishers   New York 10016

To Paul W. F. Witt

Library of Congress Cataloging in Publication Data
Wileman, Ralph E.
  Exercises in visual thinking.

  Bibliography: p.
  Includes index.
1. Visual education.   2.   Slides (Photography)
3.   Sign and symbols.   I.   Title.
LB1043.5.W497   001.55′3   79–16487
ISBN 8038–7212–7

Published simultaneously in Canada by Copp Clark, Ltd., Toronto

Designed by Al Lichtenberg
Printed in the United States of America

Table of Contents

List of Figures

FIGURE CREDITS:

Figure 50: Denoyer-Geppert

Figures 30, 33, 34 and 39 were developed under terms of a DHEW Contract No. 271–75–1016.

Preface

Visualizing educational messages is both work and play. It is work when you expend energy. It is play when you enjoy what you are doing. I hope it will be work and play for you as you go through this book.

As a teacher I have encountered many hundreds of students. They have all exhibited growth in their ability to think visually. Their energy is boundless, their commitment is absolute and their interest is intense.

Every former student made a contribution to this book. Many are now colleagues and friends. My thanks are extended to them all.

The following people helped with this book: Amy Arrendale, Doria Howe, David Ripperton, Mari Clark, Jiri Bezdek, David Haynes, Mary Allen, Alice Isley, James Henry, Betsy Murray and Ruth de Bliek.

Betty Cleaver was a supportive colleague and reader.

Lou Roser of the North Carolina Department of Public Instruction's Materials Review and Evaluation Center helped me look for quality visual aids.

Significant editorial and graphic design work was done by Cora Harrison and Steven Burke. Working with them is indeed a pleasure.

Ann, Laura and John were helpful and supportive as this book took shape.

If you find the ideas and exercises in this book helpful, I would like very much to hear from you.

Ralph E. Wileman
Peabody Hall
University of North Carolina
Chapel Hill, NC 27514

Introduction
and Glossary

This book is intended to help teachers, instructional design specialists, educational media personnel, instructional materials producers and all others interested in visual communication to improve their skill in visualizing educational messages.

There are many references, texts and periodicals that deal with graphic design and commercial art. Schools of design and visual arts teach courses in layout, composition, color, lettering and the like. Few if any of these resources and courses bear directly on improving the quality of the instructional materials used in educational settings. Even though there are beautiful children's books (e.g., the Caldecott Award winners) and attractive multi-colored packages for many learning kits, we find the visual communication aspect of most instructional materials wanting.

There are many audiovisual texts and references about the local production of instructional materials. These publications focus on the medium, where to find it, how to use it, and how to produce it. These are useful skills. However, communicators/teachers need to develop skills in visualizing, too. This book will provide the reader basic knowledge and skills in visualizing educational messages. The following terms are used throughout this book. These words should become part of the reader's working vocabulary.

Abstract Representation: An attempt to invent unique words or images to present information. Often these attempts become established and recognizable.

Audience/Learner: The individual or group for whom one is designing an educational message. The recipients of instruction.

Communicator/Teacher: Instructional planners, educational media specialists, curriculum leaders, and all those responsible for the direction of learning in academic or other educational settings.

Conceptualize: The process of inventing visual and/or verbal symbols to communicate a message. The process involves both thought and visual design skills. To storyboard, to rough draft, to sketch, to construct a mock-up.

Concrete Representation: An attempt to be literal and realistic in the presentation of information.

Educational Message Designer: Teachers, instructional planners, media specialists, curriculum leaders, and all those who are responsible for planning instruction and developing accompanying materials in academic or other educational settings.

Generalization: A conclusion or "truth" underlying a field of inquiry. Often a generalization is the result of a great deal of reflective thinking.

Graph Format: One of five ways to present tabular data: line, bar, circle, pictorial, or map/area.

Graphic: A vivid, "clean," simple visual representation of an object, concept or feeling.

Invisible Idea: A generalization or theory that has no outward visible manifestation.

Message: The visual and verbal information being transmitted from the communicator/teacher to the audience/learner.

"Read": Seeing with the eyes and understanding that which is seen.

Render: The process that turns a conceptualized message into a usable finished product. To prepare art for slides, to record, to construct a display.

Storyboard: The visual and verbal plan for an audiovisual presentation, usually slide presentations, television or motion pictures.

Symbol: An attempt to represent something.
>   *Pictorial Symbol:* A symbol using photographs or illustrations to represent (usually realistic).
>   *Graphic Symbol:* A symbol using simple, bold, shape oriented images to represent (sometimes realistic).
> > *Image Related Graphic:* A symbol designed to represent an object in a highly recognizable form. Often, it takes the form of an accurate silhouette or profile.
> > *Concept Related Graphic:* A symbol designed to represent the essence of an object. It has less detail than an image related graphic.
> > *Arbitrary Graphic:* A symbol that is purely geometric or abstract. It does not look like the object being represented.
>   *Verbal Symbol:* A symbol using words to either describe or label an object or thing.

Theory: A verified or conjectured formulation about an underlying artistic or scientific principle.

Thumbnail Sketch: A small, quickly drawn pictorial or graphic image. Used in the early planning stages of a project.

Verbalization: The process of using words to describe and represent objects, concepts or feelings.

Visible Idea: An object, thing or concept that has a pictorial or graphic counterpart.

Visual Aid: A pictorial or graphic representation of information intended to communicate. The representation may or may not include verbal cues to meaning.

Visual Communication: The attempt by human beings to use pictorial and graphic symbols to express ideas and to teach people in and out of the school setting.

Visual Literacy: The ability to "read" and understand that which is seen and the ability to generate materials that have to be seen to be understood.

Visual Thinking: Organizing mental images around shapes, lines, colors, textures and compositions.

Visualization: The process of graphically or pictorially representing objects, concepts or feelings.

1

Visual Communication

We need to communicate with each other about our world and our responses to it. Objects, processes, data, concepts, theories, feelings—the components of our experience—can be described and discussed by verbal means, both spoken and written. The components of our world and our experience can also be illuminated and presented through visual means, in a wide range of formats and media. We can articulate our knowledge and our thoughts both verbally and visually, and in doing so inform and educate each other.

However, more often than not, we feel more comfortable as verbal rather than visual communicators. The reason for this may be that we are *trained* in the use of verbalization from our earliest days. Our constant exposure to the spoken and written word as a means to share information—and its long dominance among educational techniques—has led us to assume that verbalization is the most effective means by which to communicate. The verbalization skills of writing and reading have been made the foundation of learning, and the majority of the primary school day is spent either teaching children to read or teaching subject matter to children through the spoken or written word.

The ability to share knowledge through verbal techniques is a skill of inestimable benefit to humans, and its value cannot be reasonably disputed in or out of the classroom. Verbalization, however, is not the only mode through which we can learn. The emphasis on reading and writing in our educational system suggests that verbalization is prerequisite to all learning and, perhaps, to most communication. The long experience of mankind suggests otherwise, as does the major premise of this book: that the visualization of information can be invaluable in helping the communicator/teacher teach and the audience/learner learn, and can be so whether it is used alone or accompanied by verbal information.

Despite the fact that we *see* our world more than we speak or read of it, we are rarely trained in the use of visualization, i.e., communicating messages visually. As a result, our ability to communicate is limited, for we must be as familiar with the visual realm as with the verbal if we are to communicate the richness of our experience and the complexity of our knowledge.

There are three major reasons for using visualization in communicating information:

1. *A visual message can be attention-getting.* A dynamic visual display demands attention. Attention is the first step in communicating.

2. *A visual message can be efficient.* A visual display can communicate quickly and boldly and, consequently, hasten comprehension of the message, especially when this calls for action in space or movement.

3. *A visual message can be effective.* A visual display has the capacity to produce the desired outcome. If the communicator/teacher wants the audience/learner to focus on a particular aspect of a comprehensive message, the visual display is designed with that specific focus in mind.

The potential for visual communication to affect learning in and out of school seems to portend well for the future. However, it is the author's judgment that at the present time there is a dearth of truly imaginative and appropriate visual learning materials. Of the materials that do exist, many are mere visualizations of the obvious or are poorly conceptualized visual messages. (Even a message that needs visualization can be made confusing if it is poorly designed.) Hopefully, this book will go beyond the visualization of the known or the obvious and challenge the communicator/teacher— who may often wear the hat of the educational message designer— to generate original, well-conceived visualizations that would improve and inspire learning of a particular subject.

Visualization as a New Language

Communication implies there is a message sender and a message receiver. Today, communication can be transmitted from sender to receiver through channels or media that can accommodate visual as well as verbal symbols. The fact that we say "I see" when we understand and we say "show me an example," "draw me a picture," or "describe it for me," are all indicators of our willingness to learn through visual communication. We readily accept visual messages.

We should, therefore, be willing to exploit visual communication in the educational setting by either selecting the most effective visual materials the market place has to offer *or* developing new materials "from scratch" when the market place offers a void.

Visualization, like verbalization, creates a language out of its elements, structure, and uses and, like any language, can serve infinite communicational needs. Gyorgy Kepes states that "The visual language is capable of disseminating knowledge more effectively than almost any other vehicle of communication." [1] If this language is to communicate effectively, and is to offer the viewer more than just a non-verbal image, it must present a visual message that can be understood by the viewer. (Communication can be judged successful *only* when it conveys the information it sets out to convey. This is as true for visual modes as it is for verbal modes.) Educational message designers—be they teachers, audiovisual specialists, or communicators in whatever field—must be familiar with the methods by which various types of information can be interpreted and presented visually. Viewers—the audience, learners regardless of age and level—must be taught to "read" the language of visual messages just as they are taught to read verbal messages. It is necessary that both designers and viewers be as literate visually as they are literate verbally.

We know that visualization can be applied to a wide range of messages. The following list clarifies the range of educational messages to which we could apply visualization in textbooks, slides, filmstrips, films, overhead transparencies, exhibits and the like:

1. The visual representation of concrete facts (e.g., the major types of energy resources).

2. The visual representation of directions (e.g., the steps a learner goes through to make bread). Examples here are "how-to-do-its."

3. The visual representation of processes (e.g., the steps that industry goes through to make steel). Examples here help the learner understand a procedure without necessarily having to perform the procedure.

4. The visual representation of a bit of data (e.g., the racial make-up of Mexico).

5. The visual representation of comparative data (e.g., comparing children, young adults, and mature adults as to their use of various drugs).

6. The visual representation of data recorded over time (e.g., the average rainfall in Maine for the past 100 years).

7. The visual representation of organizational structure (e.g., the U.S. State Department).

8. The visual representation of places (e.g., a map of Vatican City).

9. The visual representation of chronologies (e.g., the history of human ground transportation from the sled to the automobile).

10. The visual representation of a generalization (e.g., the investment potential of a nation).

11. The visual representation of a theory (e.g., Maslow's Holistic-Dynamic Theory).

12. The visual representation of feelings or attitudes. Examples here would be like those seen in categories 1–11, but would also reflect such things as cooperation, love, sorrow, etc. The examples would communicate both information *and* a point of view.

The enormous amount of information our society needs to communicate, coupled with the wide range of media alternatives to display that information, makes for complex choices on the part of educational message designers. As educational communicators we have moved quite slowly and cautiously in both our design and use of visualization. Bruner states that "any domain of knowledge (or any problem within that domain of knowledge) can be represented in three ways . . ." one of which is ". . . by a set of summary images or graphics that stand for a concept without defining it fully . . ." [2] With Bruner's statement as a guide, the communicator/teacher is given both the support and the challenge to visualize areas of knowledge heretofore not thought of as lending themselves to visualization. Dale describes well the communicator/teacher's role in relation to visual communication. "It is in our task as teachers to make them (visual symbols) rich and strong with meaning for the student." [3] The communicator/teacher of today is charged with the task of helping learners learn through visual modes confronted in and out of school.

Visualization as a Process

In the context of this book, visualization is considered primarily as a process and secondarily as a product. The communicator/teacher working as a designer of educational materials must intelligently and intuitively grapple with a message *before* arriving at a visual solution.

Designing educational materials in any medium calls for a great deal of thought. Many articles in educational periodicals have such titles as "An Easy Way to Make _____," or "You Too Can Have

[1] Gyorgy Kepes, *Language of Vision* (Chicago: Paul Theobald, 1964), p. 13.
[2] Jerome S. Bruner, *Toward a Theory of Instruction* (Cambridge, Massachusetts: The Belknap Press of Harvard University Press, 1966), p. 44.
[3] Edgar Dale, *Audio-Visual Methods of Teaching* (revised edition: New York: The Dryden Press, 1954), p. 310.

Fun Making _____," or "A Quick Way to Make _____." Emphasis on the making of a product gives the communicator/teacher a misleading view of how materials really should be developed.

Actually, it is the *conceptualization* and not the rendering of the materials that makes the most effective educational product. Conceptualization is the intellectual process by which you invent ways to visualize messages. Rarely is it "easy, fun or quick" to visualize a message. The "quick, easy, fun" syndrome should be eliminated from any discussion of the process. Good visual materials created for learning can take hours to conceptualize (design) and hours to render (become manifest in some format). Conceptualizing and rendering are two different and difficult tasks. Not all people can accomplish these tasks and those who can must use a great deal of their creative energy.

Preusser says that "from inception to completion, visual invention and organization are a series of decisive actions determined by instinctive and acquired knowledge." [4] Visual message design requires a great amount of mental and physical action that depends on intelligent decision making through every stage of the process.

Yes, generating new materials is an arduous task. However, this is not to say that every educational message designer must run about in sack cloth because his or her task is so time-consuming and difficult. Quite the contrary; creating new visual educational materials can be challenging and—when the learner shows evidence of learning—very rewarding.

Though some of what educational message designers do is instinctive or intuitive, much of what is done is based on knowledge and ability learned in the study of the process of visualization. One function of this book, therefore, is to stimulate or rekindle your instinctive ability to visualize. Another function is to give you—as an educational message designer—knowledge and practice regarding the conceptualization of visual messages in order to ultimately create effective, efficient, attention-getting educational materials.

Using This Book

At many points while using this book you will be asked to respond. The majority of the responses asked for will require you to sketch. It is therefore suggested that you have paper and pencil or pen on hand as you read. The majority of responses you will be asked to make will require you to conceptualize a message in a visual form—you are to come up with the visual idea.

[4] Robert Preusser, "Visual Education for Science and Engineering Students," *Education of Vision,* edited by Gyorgy Kepes (New York: George Braziller, 1965), p. 219.

An efficient way to explore alternative visual ideas is to do thumbnail sketches. (See Figure 1.) So, when given a problem, try to come up with *several* alternative ways to display the information visually. The exercise of conceptualizing alternatives should contribute to the development of your ability to think visually.

Most media—filmstrips, television, slides, overhead transparencies, publications of all types—have the potential to accommodate the visual aspect of a message. The explanation of the advantages and disadvantages of alternative media is a major task not undertaken here. In other words, this book will not help you decide the medium to use in order to display a visual message.

The task of this book is to explore alternative visual answers to given educational content. The intent of the book is to develop your "visual thinking" as well as your skills and confidence regarding visual communication for teaching and learning purposes.

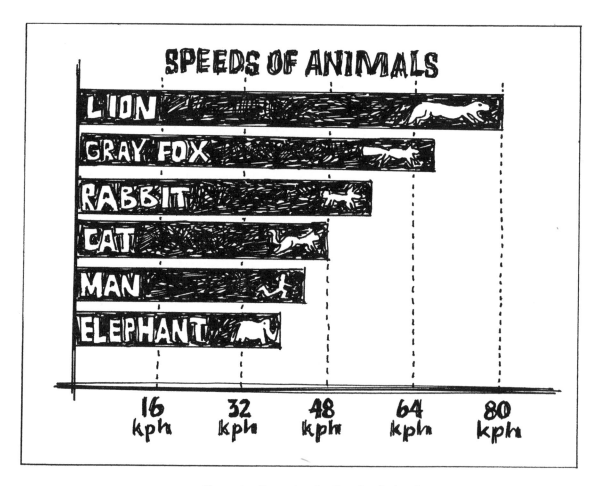

Figure 1. Example of a thumbnail sketch

Information or data contained in a box comprises an EXERCISE. You will be asked to respond to an EXERCISE with thumbnail sketches. You will also be told what page to turn to in this book to see possible alternative answers to the visual problems posed.

2 The Visual Image

We are surrounded by objects, some part of the natural environment and some man-made. Objects have always been central to our lives and our communication with each other has always been largely concerned with them—with concrete things, with matter, with nouns. Early humans carved or painted on cave walls those things they knew—things such as the family, animals and their natural environment. These early renderings were used to store facts and to communicate ideas. To be effective, the images had to be "read" just as we read words on the printed page today. For the most part these images were drawn realistically and could be easily understood. Some of these early images developed into more abstract shapes that evolved into the letters or hieroglyphics used for written communication.

This chapter will focus on developing the visual image for objects that surround us. It will concentrate on ways to visually represent objects because much of what we want an audience/learner to understand involves highly visible things. (See Figure 2.)

There are three major ways to represent objects—as *pictorial symbols, graphic symbols* and *verbal symbols.* (The representation of one object by another object is a symbol.)

Pictorial symbols are produced as either 3-D models, relief sculpture, photographs, illustrations or drawings. All of these are attempts to reconstruct the object or thing as a highly realistic/concrete symbol. The viewer should be able to transfer a pictorial symbol to reality with ease. That is, when the learner sees a pictorial symbol of a pomegranate we want him or her to be able to identify a pomegranate when a real one is confronted in the supermarket.

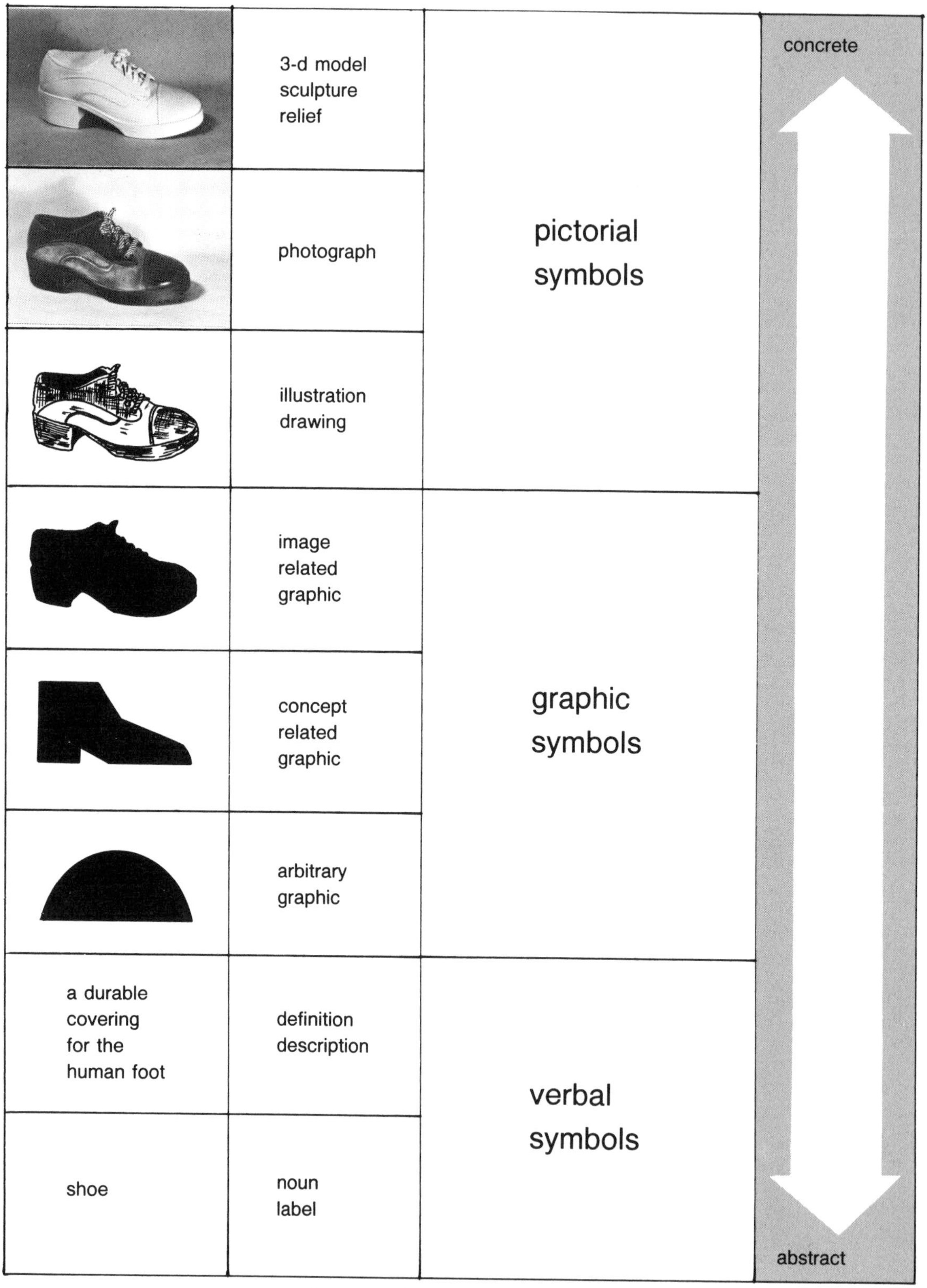

	3-d model sculpture relief		concrete
	photograph	pictorial symbols	
	illustration drawing		
	image related graphic		
	concept related graphic	graphic symbols	
	arbitrary graphic		
a durable covering for the human foot	definition description		
shoe	noun label	verbal symbols	abstract

Figure 2.   Ways to represent objects

Graphic symbols are constructed in a variety of ways. Modley [5] suggests there are three major categories of graphic symbols: *image related* graphics, *concept related* graphics and *arbitrary* graphics.

Image related graphics can best be characterized as silhouettes or profiles of the object. The object becomes flat but remains highly recognizable. *Concept related* graphics look like the object but have less detail than image related graphics. Concept related graphics are the essence of the object; they are a stylized version of the real thing. *Arbitrary* graphics are abstract symbols for an object. At times, arbitrary graphics take the form of pure geometric shapes. They are constructed out of the designer's imagination and are, as their names implies, unrelated visually to the object. They are judged successful on almost purely aesthetic grounds.

Verbal symbols are single words or whole sentences. We either use nouns to label objects or we string words together to define or describe an object. Verbal symbols can be understood only by people who have been taught the language.

The three major symbol groupings help cluster the range of ways we visually represent objects. This range is best described as running from concrete to abstract representations. Pictorial symbols are usually highly realistic, very concrete. Graphic symbols may or may not be easily read. Verbal symbols come to us in many languages, and when we hear or read a language we do not know, we become aware of just how abstract verbal symbols can be.

We use pictorial, graphic, and verbal symbols in a wide range of media from motion picture film to the printed page. The choice of symbols is directly related to our major objectives as the communicator of specific information and to our audience's ability and interests. The educational message designer should be equally adept at designing symbols at all points along the continuum of possibilities.

We have considerable technological help in producing symbols at the concrete end of the continuum. This help comes to us in the form of 35 mm cameras, laser projectors, television cameras, as well as accomplished artists who can render highly realistic paintings, drawings or 3-D models.

Likewise, we have considerable experience and ability in producing symbols at the abstract end of the continuum. We are constantly using and abusing verbal symbols in the academic forum.

We seem to need the most help in inventing images to use in the graphic symbol range on the continuum. Henry Dreyfuss has compiled a significant reference tool to help us see the range of symbols that are extant. A visit with his *Symbol Sourcebook* will open your eyes to the breadth and depth of the graphic symbols already in use.

[5] As described in the following book. Andrew Wright, *Designing for Visual Aids* (New York: Van Nostrand Reinhold Company, 1970), pp. 82–83.

EXERCISE I

pictorial symbols		graphic symbols			verbal symbols
photograph	illustration	image related	concept related	arbitrary	definition
					an adult male person
					a small, furry, feline animal
					the burning of several logs
					a shelter occupied by a small number of people.

The visualization above is incomplete. There are graphic symbols missing. The graphic symbols that are given are all bold and flat. Fill in each blank space, with an appropriate symbol of your own. Working on a separate piece of paper, come up with three thumbnail sketches for each symbol. Then, transfer your best sketch to the above chart. (Note: use a blunt-tip black felt marker or black paper to achieve mass-oriented rather than line-oriented images.) After you have filled in the boxes, turn to Alternatives Ia, Ib and Ic on page 29 to see alternative solutions.

Often, however, our task is to invent or design a *new* graphic symbol. EXERCISE I will give you practice in this activity.

When you evaluate a symbol you have designed, ask the fundamental question—does the symbol communicate? Does your audience/learner "read" the symbol and interpret it as intended? If the answer is no, then redesign the symbol. At another level of questioning ask—is the symbol well designed and aesthetically pleasing? Here, taste and opinion play a strong role. Be prepared to deal with both logical and illogical responses to your work.

Logical responses are those that you deal with by changing or redesigning your symbols. For example, look at the "before" side of Figure 3. A logical criticism might be that the shapes are clumsy and disproportional. By reworking your design you could have resolved the problem as evidenced in the "after" side of Figure 3.

Before   Figure 3.   Redesigning symbols   After

Sometimes you are given criticism that is illogical and based primarily on personal whim or fancy. For example, look at Figure 4. This symbol has been designed to stand for health centers (an arbitrary graphic symbol). An illogical criticism might be that the shape looks too much like a snowflake. Do not rework your design because of this response. Perhaps every pronged round shape looks like a snowflake to your critic.

Change your design when criticism is logical and seems valid. Hold your ground when criticism is illogical or invalid. Knowing the difference is often difficult.

Many graphic design books deal with the visual elements that need attention such as: figure/ground relationships, balance, composition, color. These elements contribute to your message development and awareness of their influence can help you improve the aesthetic quality of your designs.

A good source of inspiration on the development of graphic symbols is *Form and Communication.* In this book, Diethelm gives

Figure 4.   An arbitrary graphic

examples of geometric mathematical approaches to graphic design making. The results of following his directions can lead you to designs with infinite variation.

For additional inspiration regarding the design of graphic symbols you may find the Trade Marks and Symbols section of each *Graphis Annual* to be of help. Though many of the examples in *Graphis* are logotypes and not graphic symbols, most all of them are attempts to communicate the function or ambience of an entire company or organization. The vast majority of these symbols are bold, flat and graphic. They are also the design efforts of the world's leading graphic designers.

Becoming familiar with the alternative ways to represent objects and things is fundamental to educational message designers. These alternatives must be willingly explored and pondered as you go about designing messages.

EXERCISE II will give you practice in developing designs for an object in all the various forms discussed in this chapter—from concrete to abstract.

EXERCISE II

Design a series of representations of an object of your choosing at the following seven levels on the concrete to abstract continuum:

1. photograph
2. illustration/drawing
3. image related graphic
4. concept related graphic
5. arbitrary graphic
6. definition/description
7. noun label

Compare your designs to Alternatives IIa, IIb, IIc on pages 30–32.

Your solution to EXERCISE II could be mounted on board and displayed on the wall of your studio, office or classroom as an ever-present reminder of some of the ways to represent objects as we go about the business of message design.

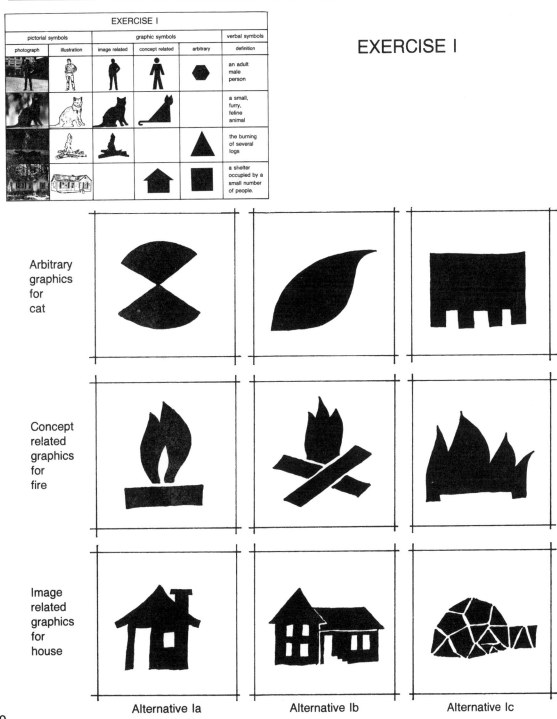

EXERCISE I					
pictorial symbols		graphic symbols			verbal symbols
photograph	illustration	image related	concept related	arbitrary	definition
					an adult male person
					a small, furry, feline animal
					the burning of several logs
					a shelter occupied by a small number of people.

EXERCISE I

Arbitrary graphics for cat

Concept related graphics for fire

Image related graphics for house

Alternative Ia   Alternative Ib   Alternative Ic

The designs presented in Alternatives Ia, Ib, and Ic, should be compatible with your designs. If they are not, perhaps you should rework your designs. Individual sketching style will make each designer's work look distinct. Your sketching style might be described as detailed, cartoony, primitive, delicate, formal or realistic. Therefore, your work need not be the *same* as the examples, only *compatible*. In other words, your image related graphic should read as a silhouette and your concept related graphic should be a very stylized version of your image related graphic. (It should represent the essence of the image, minus the details.) Your arbitrary graphic should be an abstract or pure geometric shape. (If your arbitrary graphic looks like the object or thing, then it isn't arbitrary. The image for the arbitrary graphic should be the easiest for you to invent. It may, however, be difficult to make it aesthetically pleasing. An arbitrary graphic's communicative power is closely tied to its pure design qualities.)

EXERCISE II

Alternative IIa

photograph

illustration

image related

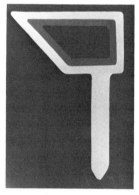

concept related

arbitrary

definition

noun

1. photograph
2. illustration/drawing
3. image related graphic
4. concept related graphic
5. arbitrary graphic
6. definition/description
7. noun label

Alternative IIb

photograph

illustration

image related

concept related

arbitrary

definition

noun

Alternative IIc

photograph

illustration

image related

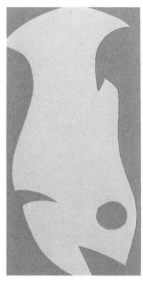

concept related

arbitrary

an aquatic
cold-blooded
animal having
fins, gills, scales
and tails of
debatable
length

definition

fish

noun

3 Words and The Visual Image

Words spoken and written play a significant part in our communication. When our message is communicated in a form other than the spoken or written word, i.e. in a visual form via slides, filmstrips, overhead transparencies or films, we are oftentimes dealing with complex relationships between words (verbal images) and pictures (visual images). Part of this complexity stems from the fact that there are many types of verbal/visual image relationships.

This chapter will focus on the verbal and the visual images that an audience or individual learner might see projected on a screen; it will not focus on the words that might accompany the projected images, which are spoken by a teacher or narrator.

Today, we find educational materials produced in a projectable media format and we are lulled into thinking they are visual aids to learning. Careful observation will reveal that in many cases learning is not aided visually because there is nothing visual at which to look. We would not call a page of typography in a book a visual aid, yet the same page photographed and projected on a screen is considered by some to be a visual aid to learning. Perhaps words on a screen are different from words on a piece of paper. Perhaps not.

To project words on a screen is not necessarily right or wrong. This technique is valid in some cases. Be aware, however, that slides composed strictly of words are not necessarily visual aids! Visual aids worthy of projection and distinctly different from the spoken or printed word are more likely to include photography, illustrations or graphic symbols along with a few significant words. Figure 5 is an attempt to organize the possible verbal/visual image relationships.

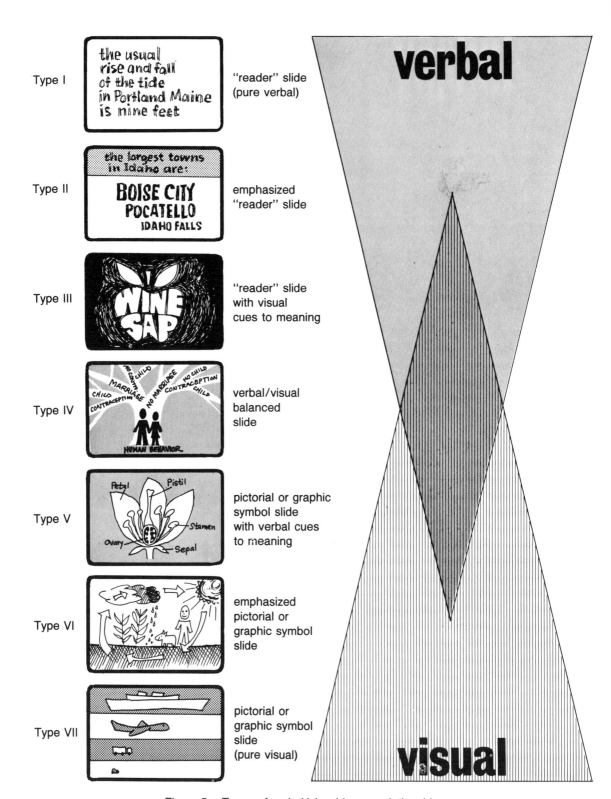

Figure 5. Types of verbal/visual image relationships

(This figure, and the description which follows, is tied directly to the slide presentation format; however, the information can be applied to any other media format where words and/or pictures are displayed.) The following is a discussion of each of the seven types of verbal/visual image relationships.

Type I—"Reader" Slide

This purely verbal presentation is closely tied in kind to the printed page. In order to comprehend the message, the viewer must be verbally literate. The designer of the message can affect the message through choice of typeface, layout of type, and use of color for the background and/or the type. "Reader" slides are often short titles, headings or lists of words. They are used to either outline ideas that will be presented in subsequent slides or to summarize or review preceding slides.

A "reader" slide should, at best, accommodate no more than 24 words; the printed page usually can accommodate 10 times that number of words. Efficiency suggests that lengthy verbal messages belong on the printed page.

Type II—Emphasized "Reader" Slide

This presentation is verbal but adds a technique we will call emphasis. Emphasis can be applied to "reader" slides in a variety of ways. Sometimes emphasis is strictly decorative as in Figure 6 where words are bordered with a filigree pattern. This example may

Figure 6.
Emphasized "reader"
slide (decorated)

be attractive and well designed, but we should ask the question, does the viewer understand the message any better because of the filigree or decorative pattern? Probably not. However, this technique can attract or captivate the viewer's attention prior to literal reading of the message. This technique may be necessary and useful and serve an instructional purpose, i.e. to aid retention of the information.

At other times, emphasis can be employed for the purpose of accenting part of the message. Accenting helps focus the viewer's attention. For example, by placing an asterisk beside two items out of five, we know on which two to focus our attention. (See Figure 7.)

Emphasizing techniques include:
- Changing the typeface for key words
- Using all upper or all lower case letters for key words
- Changing type size
- Using color
- Using decoration
- Using a star, asterisk or check beside key words

Type III—"Reader" Slide with Visual Cues to Meaning

This presentation is verbal but adds pictorial or graphic symbols that help communicate the message. To drop the words out of the side of a building (see Figure 8) tells the viewer a bit more about the conditions of deprivation.

In Figure 9 we are told verbally the subject of the presentation and we are given a visual cue to the relationship between the two elements. Development affects population and population affects development. Development and population mesh.

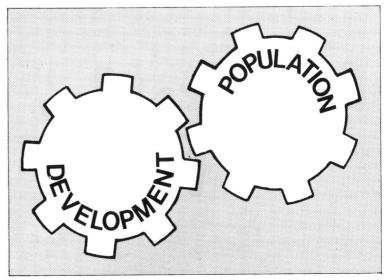

Figure 8.
"Reader" slide with visual cues to meaning (illustration)

the five major characteristics related to territoriality. The words used are few and serve to orient the viewer only. This set of graphics communicates a rather complex idea.

Likewise, this presentation type is appropriate to use for the representation of numerical data in which the message is to be visualized and the words are used only to orient the viewer. (See Figure 12.) Although the viewer has to be able to read in order to discern

Figure 9.
"Reader" slide with graphic cues to meaning

In this combined verbal/visual presentation, the viewer can receive the message in part from what is seen rather than having to totally rely on what is read. This treatment is intended to aid understanding as well as to help hold and direct attention.

Type IV—Verbal/Visual Balanced Slide

This presentation is balanced and offers the viewer the opportunity to receive the message as a verbal message or a visual message or in some combination. Figure 10 helps communicate the concept of the rain cycle as a verbal message or as a visual message or in some verbal/visual combination.

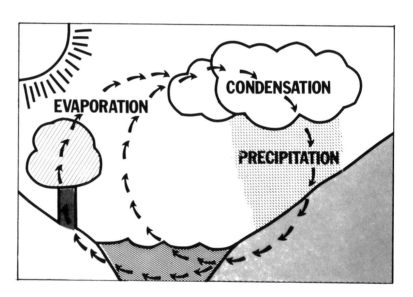

Figure 10.
Verbal/visual balanced slide

Note that the cyclical layout of the words (as opposed to a linear list) is also intended to contribute to the understanding of the message. A judicious use of words with clear meaningful graphics can intrigue the viewer and provoke a great deal of inquiry into the meaning of this message.

Type V—Pictorial or Graphic Symbol Slide with Verbal Cues to Meaning

This presentation is distinguished by the fact that the visualization of the message is primary and words are used only as landmarks or to label new or exotic phenomenon. For example, Figure 11 depicts

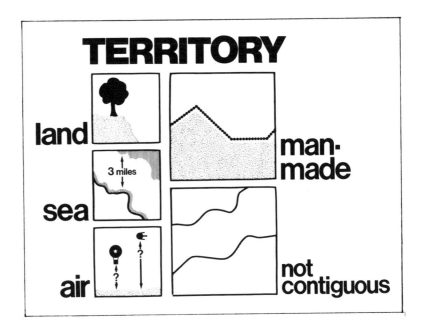

Figure 11.
Pictorial or graphic symbol
slide with verbal cues to
meaning (illustration)

the five major characteristics related to territoriality. The words used
are few and serve to orient the viewer only. This set of graphics
communicates a rather complex idea.

Likewise, this presentation type is appropriate to use for the
representation of numerical data in which the message is to be visualized and the words are used only to orient the viewer. (See Figure
12.) Although the viewer has to be able to read in order to discern

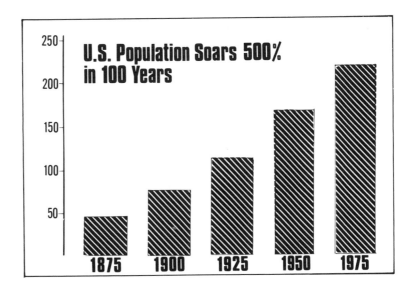

Figure 12.
Pictorial or graphic symbol
slide with verbal cues to
meaning (graphics)

the subject of this graph, the major aspect of this message comes from "reading" or interpreting the visual side of the presentation. The viewer needs to be visually literate to understand the data.

Type VI—Emphasized Pictorial or Graphic Symbol Slide

In this presentation, few words are included. For example, in Figure 13 it is clear that two parts of the jug will be the focus of our attention. Those two parts are the handle and the base. The

Figure 13.
Emphasized pictorial or graphic symbol slide

Figure 14.
Pictorial or graphic symbol
slide (photograph)

viewer must be able to "read" the emphasizing technique—in this case, circles that emphasize specific parts of a jug.

Emphasizing techniques include:

- Using arrows to point out, signal directions or show flow
- Using circles to isolate an aspect
- Using a bold or a delicate style to emphasize an aspect of the image
- Using screens, textures or colors around that which is to be emphasized
- Enlarging an aspect as if it were under a magnifying glass

Type VII—Pictorial or Graphic Symbol Slide

This presentation is purely visual. Photographs, detailed illustrations, simple graphics and geometric shapes are used to communicate the message. For example, a photograph of a *fali* (Figure 14) tells the viewer something about homes in Samoa. Likewise, the illustration of the orthopedic patient (Figure 15) is pure visual information. It is this presentation type that is used most often in slide and filmstrip presentations. The camera is used to photographically record an event, a place or an artist's rendered picture. The distinguishing

41

feature at this level seems to be the style or technique of the photographer or the renderer. For example, if the subject to be communicated is tongue and groove construction, the quality of how well this idea is communicated is directly related to the skill of the photographer or the rendering hand of the artist.

As educational message designers go about conceptualizing all kinds of content with the eventual goal of producing slides, filmstrips, exhibits or the like, it would be advisable to consider using all seven types of verbal/visual image relationships presented in this chapter. The real challenge for designers comes in utilizing a healthy mixture of the various types with emphasis on Types III, IV, and V. Again, these three types mix words and pictorial/graphic images. This mixture, for most audiences, is the most helpful in terms of learning.

A survey of extant slides and filmstrips will reveal a proponderance of Type I and Type VII presentations. For example, most slide presentations are "reader" slides, photographs or illustrations of persons, places or things. The reason for this rather easy solution to designing the visual aspect of slides or a filmstrip is that the *substance* of the message in most presentations of this kind is carried by a narration that is either read by the instructor or heard via an accompanying tape or disc recording.

Figure 15.
Pictorial or graphic symbol slide (illustration)

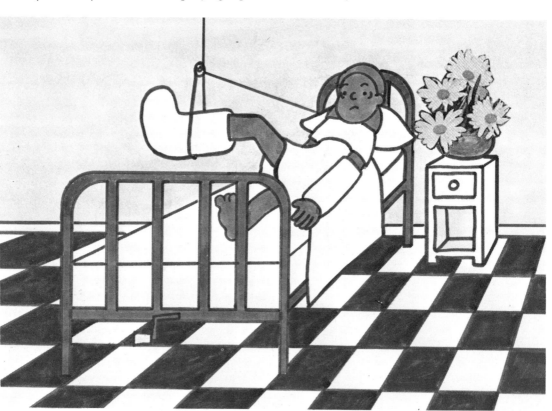

Figure 16. A storyboard

Perhaps you have heard of the "illustrated lecture." In most cases, if the lecturer forgets to bring the projector to the presentation, the audience would not be missing a great deal of the message. The slides are not nearly as important as the words that are to be heard. The lecturer could speak without his slides. But, could the slides be presented without the lecturer? Probably not.

In the above example, the message is, by design, primarily verbal and carried by the narrator. The visuals projected on the screen carry little of the weight of the message. They are, thereby, secondarily important.

This seemingly limited use of the visualization aspect of presentations could be overcome if slides and filmstrips were conceptualized on storyboards rather than in typewriters. A storyboard is a *verbal and visual plan.* (See Figure 16.) Using this technique encourages visualization during the conceptualization stage of planning. Storyboarding is a time-honored technique employed by the advertising and communications industry. Successful educational media producers also take full advantage of this planning tool. For further help in planning and storyboarding see Gerald Kemp's *Planning and Producing Audiovisual Materials.* The traditional planning technique—

the writing of scripts—emphasizes the verbal aspect of the presentation.

A well conceived presentation, no matter what the format, demands that the visual aspect of the presentation carry a significant part of the communication weight of the message. How much or how little to visualize is obviously related to the kind of message to be communicated. The variety of kinds of messages will be described and discussed in the next four chapters. Chapters IV, V, and VI ask for your participation in designing answers to communication problems that require verbal/visual message design.

To conclude this chapter, test yourself on your ability to classify verbal/or visual presentations as to their respective types.

EXERCISE III

Exercise IIIa

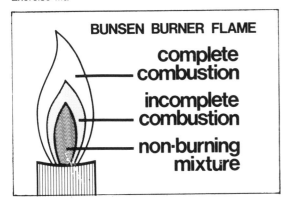

Exercise IIIb

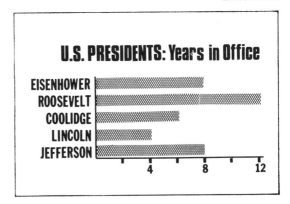

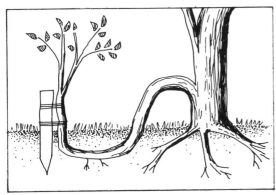

Exercise IIIc

Exercise IIId

Classify the four examples above as to the following types:

Type I—"Reader" Slide (pure verbal)

Type II—Emphasized "Reader" Slide

Type III—"Reader" Slide with Visual Cues to Meaning

Type IV—Verbal/Visual Balanced Slide

Type V—Pictorial or Graphic Symbol Slide with Verbal Cues to Meaning

Type VI—Emphasized Pictorial or Graphic Symbol Slide

Type VII—Pictorial or Graphic Symbol Slide (pure visual)

The appropriate answers are on page 46.

EXERCISE III

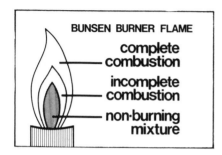

IIIa
Type V—Pictorial or graphic symbol slide
with verbal cues to meaning.
An illustration with labels.

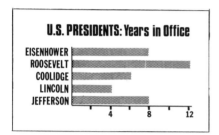

IIIb
Type V Pictorial or graphic symbol slide
with verbal cues to meaning. A labeled graph.

IIIc
Type VII—Pictorial or graphic symbol slide (pure visual).

IIId
Type II—Emphasized "reader" slide.
Use of decorative techniques.

4 The Visualization of Facts, Directions and Processes

We have all been subjected to visuals that were intended to teach us facts, directions and processes. The ubiquitous pull-down map on the wall; the illustrated cookbook; the laminated emergency directions in the seat pocket of the airplane are all attempts to communicate, at least in part, visually. How well they communicate is directly a function of how well they are designed and how well they can be "read." The visual aspect, like the verbal aspect, must be "read" if the message is to be understood or acted upon in an appropriate way.

Can you "read" Figure 17? You are able to quickly "read" Figure 17—a pictogram—if you can read the image-related graphics for match, flame, wood, bellows (air) and log fire. In addition, you must be familiar with the equation, $1/3 + 1/3 + 1/3 = 1$. Here, the viewer is guided through the message in the traditional left to right order of a simple mathematical equation; the plus sign $(+)$ and the equals mark $(=)$ are significant aids to "reading" the message.

Visual Techniques for Ordering Information

A message, in essence, is a short story. In the case of Figure 17, the message is "read" by means of a strictly visual language. And, as in any good story, the language used is bold, simple and clear. Furthermore, this visual story employs one of several techniques for ordering information, i.e. the use of mathematical symbols. The viewer's attention is actually *directed through* the content by means of the symbols.

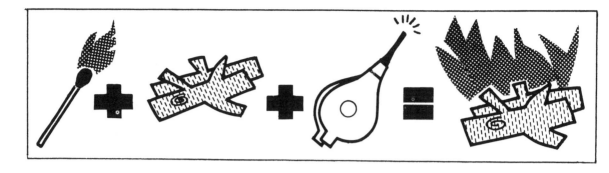

Figure 17.   Pictogram

The words "directed through" are important here because they imply that what is to be represented has a beginning and end. It also has an order—a sequence, flow or movement.

The point to be made is that when representing facts, directions or processes, it is often appropriate to order information into a sequence, movement or flow.

Aside from mathematical symbols used above, arrows, numbers and graduated screens are other valuable techniques for ordering information.

Figure 18 indicates how the arrow can be used to show movement of information. Note that the viewer follows the arrow in a direction opposite the top-to-bottom orientation traditionally used to present a verbal message on a printed page.

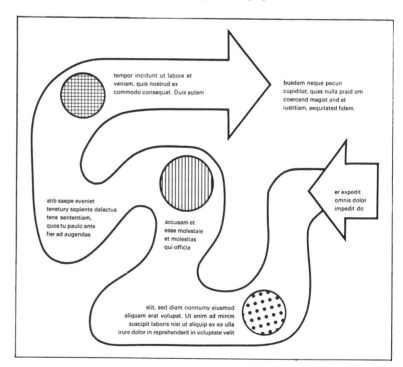

Figure 18.
Arrow directing flow of attention

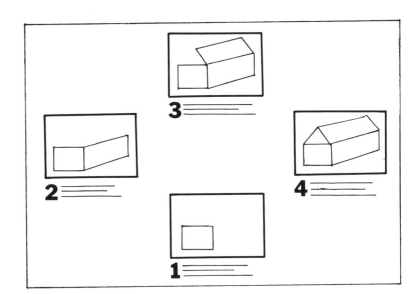

Figure 19.
Numbers directing the flow
of attention

Figure 19 uses numbers to move the viewer through sequential information. The viewer is forced to read the numbers in a less than traditional fashion. Note that in this case, the numbers must be large or else the viewer will, by custom, start "reading" in the upper left hand corner.

Figure 20 is an example of how movement is created by the graduated shading of the background. Light to dark seems to be the direction in which most people read screens; however, gradual shading may be employed so that the viewer's attention is directed from dark to light, as in this case.

Figure 20.
Shading directing the flow
of attention

Employ arrows, numbers or graduated screens as techniques to help visualize the flow of information in EXERCISE IV.

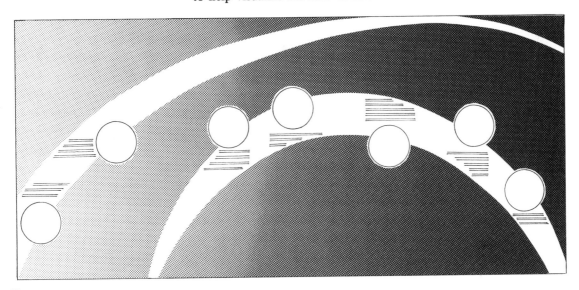

EXERCISE IV

The idea is to give the beginning cook directions on how to dice potatoes:

1. Wash the potato (with a brush and water)
2. Peel the potato (with a peeler)
3. Cut slabs 1/4" (with a knife)
4. Chop squares (with a chopper)
5. Results: ready-to-use diced potatoes

Rough sketch a visual display of directions on how to dice potatoes. The display could be for a cookbook, or a chart that hangs in the home economics laboratory or kitchen. The important aspect of this EXERCISE is to challenge you to help the viewer see the flow or direction of the steps.

When you finish, refer to Alternative IVa and IVb and IVc on page 59 for other ways to show movement/flow.

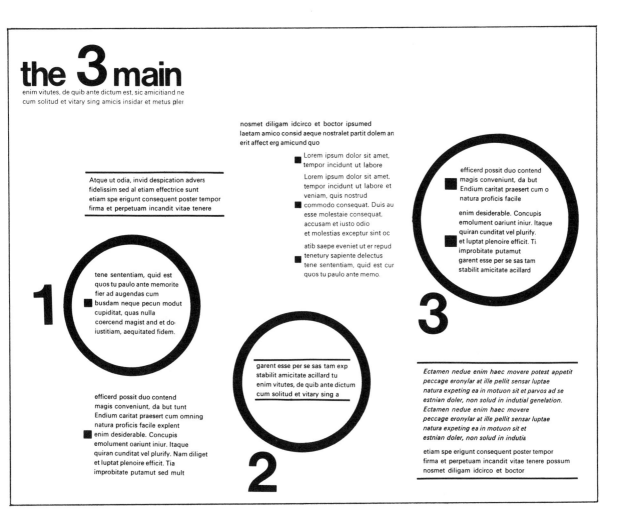

Figure 21.
Circles used to highlight

Visual Techniques for Highlighting Information

Often, in order to represent facts, directions or processes, it is appropriate to highlight an important point or series of points. Several visual techniques can be employed. Circles, other geometric shapes and asterisks can be used to highlight. In Figure 21, note that three main parts are circled in order to orient the viewer.

Screens and textures can be used to highlight an aspect of the message. In Figure 22, the viewer is *forced* to look at the two areas

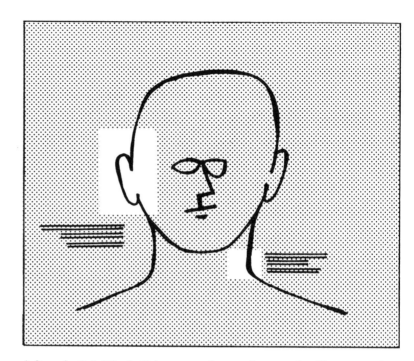

Figure 22.
Shading used to highlight

left unshaded. The judicious use of one color can also direct attention to those areas.

Blowups pull the significant information forward for close observation as in Figure 23. Note that this magnification of detail could be visualized by itself. However, the addition of "background" information helps the viewer "read" the entire story—in context.

To explore ways of highlighting information, try your hand at EXERCISE V.

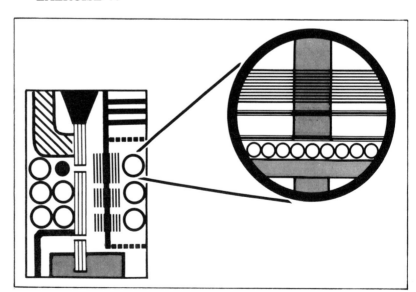

Figure 23.
Blowup used to highlight

EXERCISE V

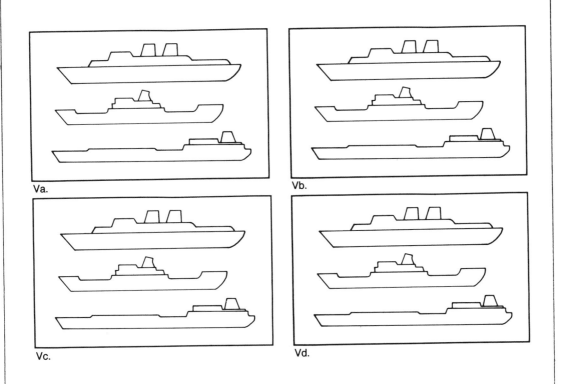

Va.

Vb.

Vc.

Vd.

Refer to the four-part visualization above. As you can see, the same three ships are repeated four times.

Highlight only the *top* ship in each of the four segments. Make each attempt to highlight different from the next. Do not use words.

Plan and sketch ways to highlight. Then, with pencil, pen or felt marker, work directly on the visualization above. When you have finished, refer to Alternative V on page 60 for other ways to highlight.

To improve your ability you must practice. The following series of exercises gives you an opportunity to improve your ability to think visually.

FACTS

There are many ways to represent objects and things. These ways were discussed in detail in Chapter II. Valid information about specific objects and things makes up what we call facts. Facts deemed worthy of considering and worthy of learning are worthy of visualizing.

EXERCISE VI will give you practice in visualizing facts. Incorporate the techniques of highlighting in working out your solutions.

EXERCISE VI

Doric   Ionic   Corinthian

Refer to the visualization above. Prepare a rough sketch for a handout that communicates the differences and similarities among the three types of Greek columns: Ionic, Doric, and Corinthian.

Audience: 10th graders

Objectives:

1) The learners will be able to label the three types of columns when given a drawing of each type.
2) The learners will describe one common characteristic of the three structures.
3) The learners will be able to name the unique characteristic of each column.

After you have sketched a plan, refer to Alternative VIa, VIb, and VIc on page 61 for comparative ideas.

DIRECTIONS

Often educators have to teach learners "how to," such as: how to wire a circuit, how to make corn muffins, or how to finger-paint. Visualization can help assure learning of these skills.

At times, directions for "how to do it" require the learner to perform motor skill acts. Photographs and line drawings are the most common ways to represent directions.

Many directions are depicted with hands performing the acts of skill. Figures 24 and 25 are photographs of the same event, chopping cabbage. Note that each picture has a different visual point of view of the event. Figure 24 is a third person point of view, that is, the viewer is looking at someone chopping cabbage. The viewer is watching a performance of the act of chopping. Figure 25 is a first person point of view, that is, the viewer seems to be looking at himself/herself chopping cabbage. The viewer is performing the act of chopping. (Current theory suggests that the first person approach is the more desirable choice when teaching people a new set of directions to follow.)

EXERCISE VII will give you practice in representing directions. Incorporate the techniques for demonstrating order, movement and flow in your solutions. Also, maintain a consistent point of view in your visualization.

Figure 24. Third person point of view

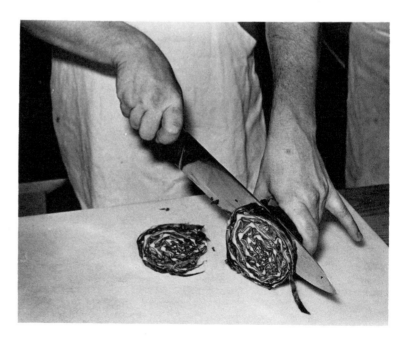

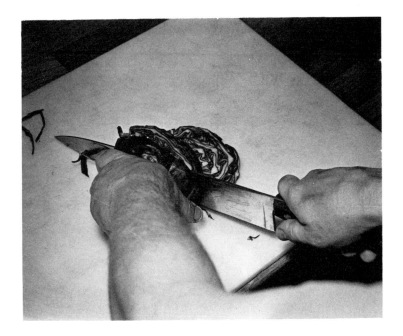

Figure 25. First person point of view

EXERCISE VII

Prepare a rough design for a poster on how to start a pepper plant indoors. Here are the verbal directions to be visualized.

- With a pencil, punch three holes in the bottom of a paper or styrofoam cup.
- Fill the cup almost full with equal parts of soil and mica, mixed.
- Plant one pepper seed down 1/2″ from the top.
- Cover the seed.
- Water.
- Place in warm sun—water daily.
- You should have a plant "sprout" in 6–8 days.

Audience: 5th graders

Objective: The learner will be able to successfully start a pepper plant indoors (for ultimate transplanting outdoors)

After you have roughed out a layout, turn to Alternatives VIIa, VIIb, and VIIc on page 62 for other solutions.

PROCESSES

Sometimes we want learners to understand a process without necessarily expecting them to go through the process. We want them to be oriented to the process, have general knowledge about it, or be motivated to take part in the process at a later date. For example, it might be necessary to introduce the learner to the process of how a verbal communication is transferred from New York to California via the telephone, or the process a health claim goes through before payment is made, or the process of finding a new job.

The following EXERCISE will give you practice in representing processes.

EXERCISE VIII

Prepare a rough design for a wall display, that will communicate the process of giving blood at the local hospital. The process takes 45 minutes and involves the following steps:

a) Give personal data (medical history).
b) Test for type and health of blood
    (finger prick).
c) Clean arm.
d) Draw blood.
e) Rest for 15 minutes.
f) Eat snack.
g) Resume normal activity
    (no stressful activities for 24 hours).

Audience: Adults

Objectives:

1) The learner will be able to name the steps in the process of giving blood.
2) The learner will be motivated to give blood at a future date.
3) The learner will be less anxious about the idea of giving blood.

After you have sketched your solution, refer to Alternatives VIIIa, VIIIb, and VIIIc on page 63 for comparative approaches.

The visualization of facts, directions and processes is necessary if we are to communicate. Hopefully, this chapter has started you thinking about alternative ways to make the visualization of facts, directions and processes more stimulating and comprehensible to the viewer.

EXERCISE IV

1. Wash the potato (with a brush and water)
2. Peel the potato (with a peeler)
3. Cut slabs 1/4″ (with a knife)
4. Chop squares (with a chopper)
5. Results: ready-to-use diced potatoes

wash with a brush   peel   cut in slabs   chop   diced potatoes

IVa.   Illustrations in a shaded background direct flow of attention.

IVb.   Concept related graphics in an arrow direct attention.

IVc.   Numbered photographs direct attention flow.

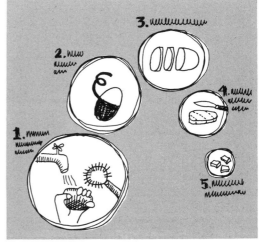

EXERCISE V

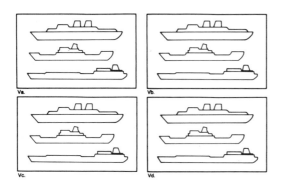

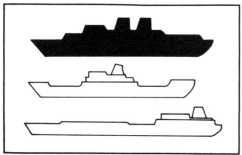

Va. Black or a color can set off an object.

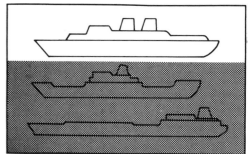

Vb. "Screening down" can deemphasize an object, emphasizing others.

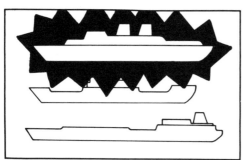

Vc. An "explosion" can highlight an object.

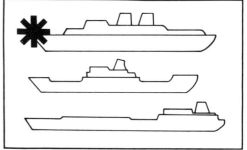

Vd. A ribbon or asterisk can single out an object.

EXERCISE VI

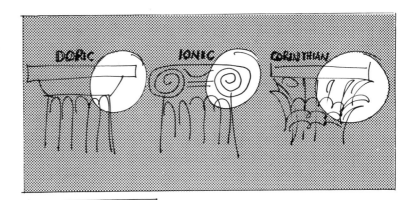

VIa.
Highlighting the unique
aspect of each column.

VIb.
A verbal/visual
cue to remembering
each type column.

VIc. Illustrates the columns are different in
both height and capital. This alternative also
"states" that one came into being before another. This kind of information may be helpful
for the learner who is interested in historic
development. (Note that, in this example, research beyond the expectations of the EXER-
CISE was performed.)

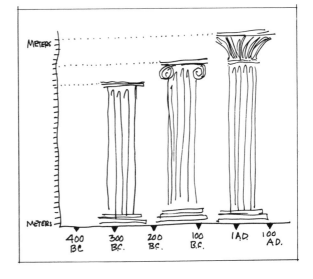

EXERCISE VII

- With a pencil, punch three holes in the bottom of a paper or styrofoam cup.
- Fill the cup almost full with equal parts of soil and mica, mixed.
- Plant one pepper seed down 1/2″ from the top.
- Cover the seed.
- Water.
- Place in warm sun—water daily.
- You should have a plant "sprout" in 6–8 days.

VIIa.
Gives directions with hands doing each step. Note the visual emphasis is on the product—the results of your work (a plant!).

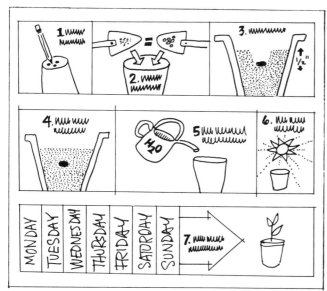

VIIb. A "classic" comic book layout. Note that all critical elements are present *except* for the hands that perform the task.

VIIc. A pictogram that weaves the steps into a story that deals with the "why" as well as the "how-to" start a plant. This method is a variation on reading, but has the pleasant addition of visual cues for the open interpretation of the viewer.

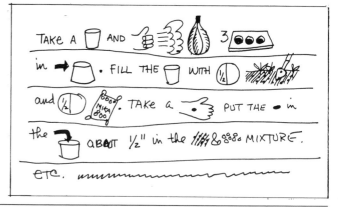

EXERCISE VIII

a) Give personal data (medical history).
b) Test for type and health of blood (finger prick).
c) Clean arm.
d) Draw blood.
e) Rest for 15 minutes.
f) Eat snack.
g) Resume normal activity (no stressful activities for 24 hours).

VIIIa. Highlights a relaxed human being.

VIIIb. Emphasis on short number of steps. Also illustrates the "everyday type" medical equipment necessary in each step.

VIIIc. An attempt to communicate that it takes less than an hour of your time to give bood. (It's quick!)

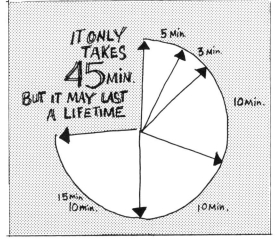

Death Rate in 1975 by Size of Landholdings, Companiganj, Bangladesh	
Size of Land Holding (Acres)	Death Rate
None	35.8
.01-.49	28.4
.50-2.99	21.5
3.00+	12.2

Source: The Johns Hopkins University School of Hygiene & Public Health, preliminary data.

Figure 26. A table

5 The Visualization of Numerical Data

"Even within a poor society, the poorest are the hardest hit. A classification of deaths in Companiganj for 1975 by a John Hopkins medical team showed that death rates differed profoundly according to the victims' land-owning status." [6] In Bangladesh, when no land is held, the death rate is 35.8, whereas those who own three or more acres have a death rate of 12.2. In between, those with less than half an acre have a death rate of 28.4; whereas owners of ½ acre up to 3 acres have a death rate of 21.5.

To a few people the above data is readable and understandable. However, the vast majority need help in organizing this information to see the significance of it. There are several ways to organize the data. The most common is a table (see Figure 26). At best, this table communicates to an exclusive audience but remains a confusing morass of data to the general public. Numerical information is usually too complex and unfamiliar for the majority of people to understand clearly.

Perhaps it would be more helpful to present data in the form of a visualization—in this case commonly called a graph. There are many ways to do this. Figures 27 and 28 are two ways the tabular data seen in Figure 26 can be visually represented. Each demonstrates boldly and succinctly that as land ownership increases in Bangladesh, the death rate decreases.

This chapter will focus on alternative approaches to dealing with numerical data with the aim of breathing life into the statistics that are generated in every professional community.

[6] Lester R. Brown, *World Population Trends: Signs of Hope, Signs of Stress,* (Washington, D.C.: Worldwatch Institute, 1976), p. 20.

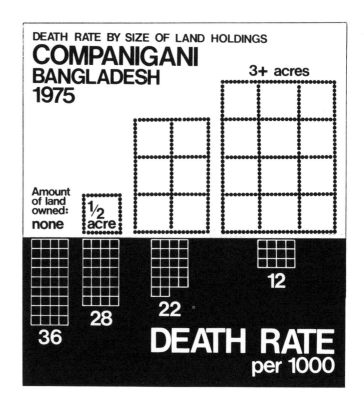

Figure 27.   A line graph

Figure 28.   An area graph

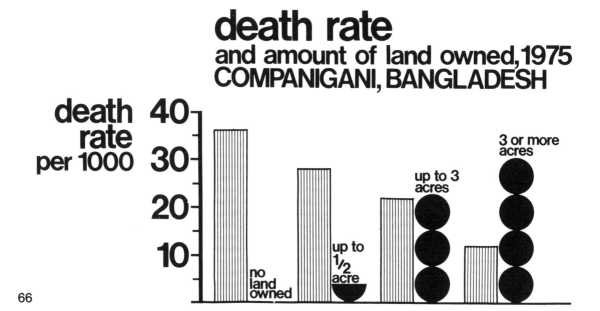

The Graph

The fact that a graph can make a general statement is its greatest strength. A visual display cannot, and should not, be as explicitly detailed as a table. A graph should serve to give an impression, indicate a trend or change, or convey a sense of the movement of data. This is usually all an audience needs to know. (If details or specific facts are needed there is no denying they are best retrieved from tables or prose writing.)

Regardless of the medium of presentation (printed handout, slides, filmstrip, overhead transparency, etc.) there are five well-known graph formats from which to choose:

- circle graph
- line graph
- bar graph
- pictorial graph
- map/area graph

These formats are not mutually exclusive and are often combined in order to satisfy specific objectives. Before a selection can be made regarding which graph format is most appropriate for a particular message, it is important to become acquainted with each format and its individual advantages.

CIRCLE GRAPH

The circle graph, commonly called a pie graph, is an appropriate format to employ when the numerical data are to be stated in terms of a total, a whole—100%. (See Figure 29.) For instance, circle graphs are useful when information concerns a total age group, all members of a single sex or a total population.

Figure 29.   The circle graph

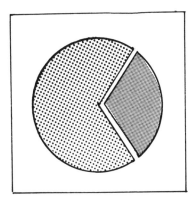
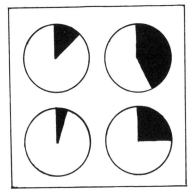
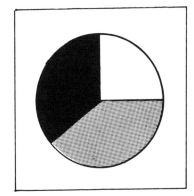

A circle graph is always divided into segments. Simple line patterns, tones of gray or color should be applied to these individual segments to create visual separations. Thus, relationships between segments are highlighted; likewise, comparisons of all segments relative to the whole are equally clear. More than one circle can be used in a visualization to emphasize further relationships and comparisons.

Circle graphs should be utilized only if each segment or "piece of the pie" will be large enough to "read." Too many variables will make the segments too small and render the graph useless in communicating data to an audience.

The circle graph is a good choice in Figure 30 since it is as important to visualize how many students *use* marijuana as it is to show how many *do not use* marijuana. The gray tones are subtly graduated and actually overlap each other demonstrating, visually and quantitatively, the *addition* of data. The gray tones deepen as the next user-category is added, thus suggesting that more users are being included in a particular category.

Figure 31 incorporates two ideas using circle graphs. It shows, 1) the percentage of men versus the percentage of the women and, 2) the proportional increase in the size of the total populations over time (shown by the change in size of the circles).

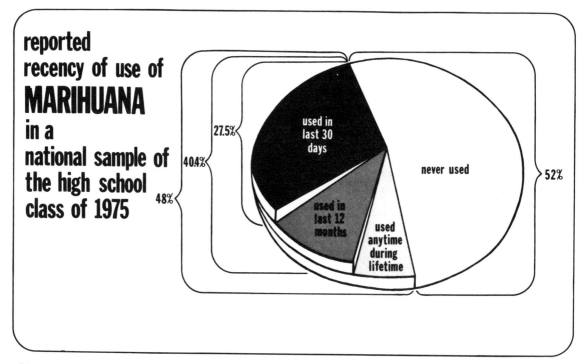

Figure 30.   Circle graph of marijuana use

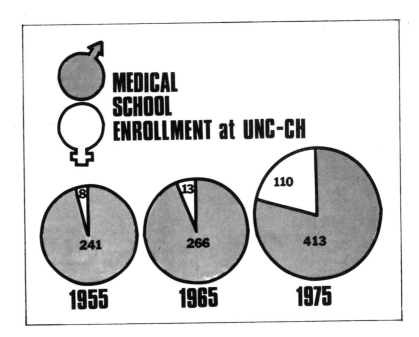

Figure 31. Circle graph
of changes over time

LINE GRAPH

The line graph is a functional technique to employ when displaying the overall movement of numerical data over a definite period of time. (See Figure 32.) Using this format, large amounts of data can be presented in a single display—the flow of events over centuries can be visualized with as much clarity as events occurring within the past twelve months. The line graph is a format that can demonstrate the fluctuations, highs and lows, rapid or slow movements, or relative stability of statistics. In addition, the line graph is an excellent format to utilize when comparisons and relationships need to be communicated. Line graphs can incorporate two, three, four, or more scales to compare the same item in different time periods.

Figure 32. A line graph

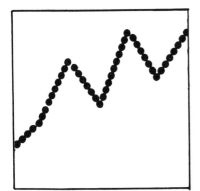
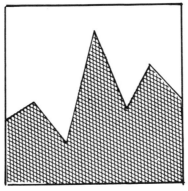
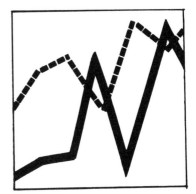

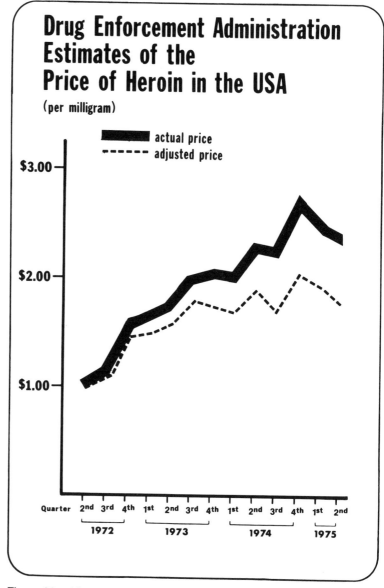

Figure 33. Line graph illustrating changes over time

Figure 33 uses the line graph format to show the movement of the price of heroin over a four-year period. First, the eye is drawn to "read" the bold black scale. A second scale (dotted line) is incorporated so that a more complete and accurate economic story is communicated to the viewer. The message of the graph now becomes clear; although the price of heroin is rising sharply, it is rising in line with general inflationary prices.

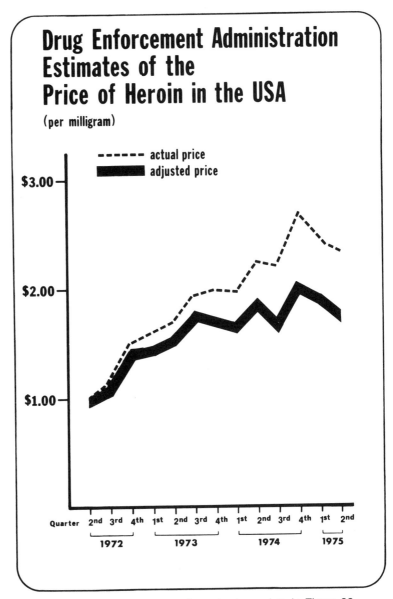

Figure 34. Line graph, reversed emphasis on data in Figure 33

Figure 34 visualizes the same data as Figure 33; however, the visual emphasis is reversed. This change in emphasis may come as a result of a reevaluation of audience needs and/or a reconsideration of the primary objective.

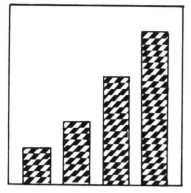  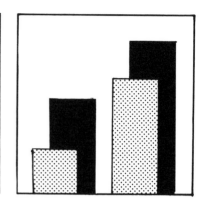

Figure 35.   A bar graph

BAR GRAPH

The bar graph is one of the most convenient and widely used formats for displaying numerical data. (See Figure 35.) The length of a bar corresponds to an item's value or amount. When a second bar is added, a comparison becomes possible. As more bars are added, more comparisons are possible.

There is a distinction between a *horizontal bar graph* and a *vertical bar graph*. The horizontal bar graph, with bars lined up horizontally, usually deals with different items compared during the same period of time. The horizontal bar graph is arranged so that items compared are listed on the vertical axis, and the quantity or amount scale is listed on the horizontal axis.

Figure 36.   A set of horizontal bar graphs

The vertical bar graph, with bars lined up vertically, deals with similar items compared at different periods of time. The vertical bar graph lists the amount scale on the vertical axis and time on the horizontal axis.

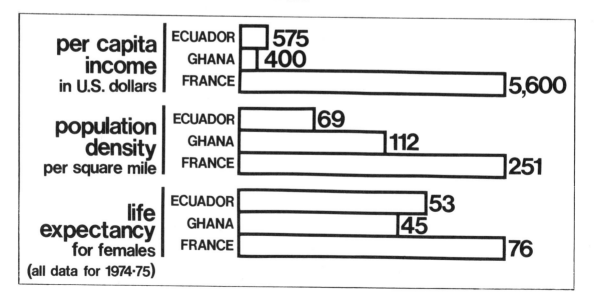

per capita income in U.S. dollars	ECUADOR	575
	GHANA	400
	FRANCE	5,600
population density per square mile	ECUADOR	69
	GHANA	112
	FRANCE	251
life expectancy for females	ECUADOR	53
	GHANA	45
	FRANCE	76

(all data for 1974·75)

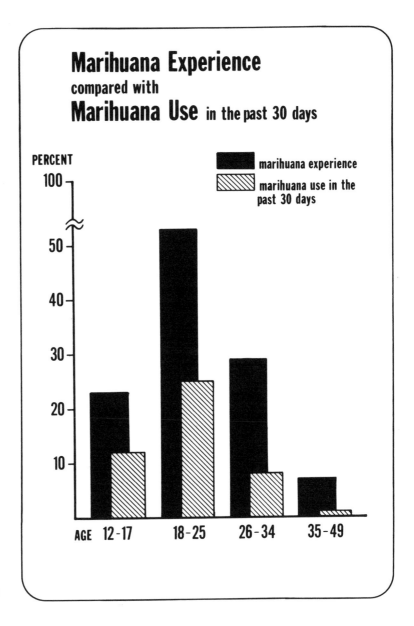

Figure 37.   A vertical bar graph

Bars can overlap each other to emphasize groupings and can employ texture and color to dramatize distinctions.

Figure 36 is a set of horizontal bar graphs that focuses on changes in quantities/percentages among different items (various countries, in this example).

Figure 37 is a vertical bar graph that encourages comparison between two consistent items (those who have ever experienced marijuana and those who have used marijuana within the past 30 days).

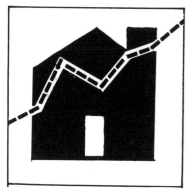  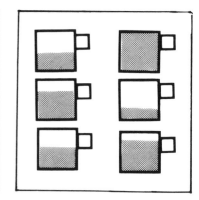

Figure 38.   A pictorial graph

PICTORIAL GRAPH

The pictorial graph uses photographs, illustrations and geometric or abstract shapes to help communicate numerical data. (See Figure 38.) These symbols take the place of conventional circles, bars and lines. Pictorial graphs incorporate symbols in two distinct ways.

First, a visual symbol can be used as an actual counting unit. Each symbol is given a specific quantitative value and becomes an integral part of the graph. An accurate reading of the graph is dependent on the translation of the symbol itself. Figure 39 is an example that uses graphic symbols in place of bars.

Figure 39.   Pictorial graph (graphics as counting units)

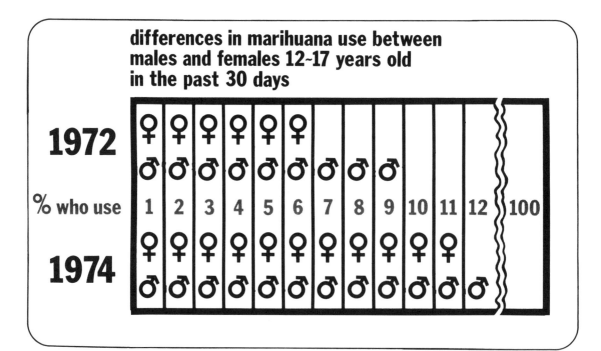

number of persons reporting adjusted gross annual income of $1,000,000 or more, 1964-1970

Figure 40. Pictorial graph
(background pictorial)

Second, a visual symbol can be used as a backdrop for statistical data presented in the more traditional bar or line graph format. Here, symbols are integrated into the graph but are not an essential part of its basic structure. The graph could conceivably be read without the symbol; however, the addition of the symbol strengthens the design and visual interest of the graph. Figure 40 uses a photograph as the background for depicting data on U.S. millionaires.

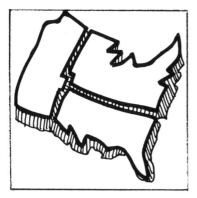 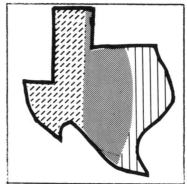 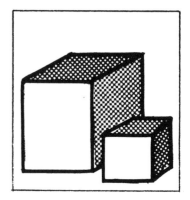

Figure 41.   A map/area graph

Because pictorial graphs offer more freedom in terms of design than any other format, care must be taken so that creative freedom does not result in visual chaos. Design appropriateness and information value must be balanced when considering pictorial representations.

Figure 42.   Line graph in a map

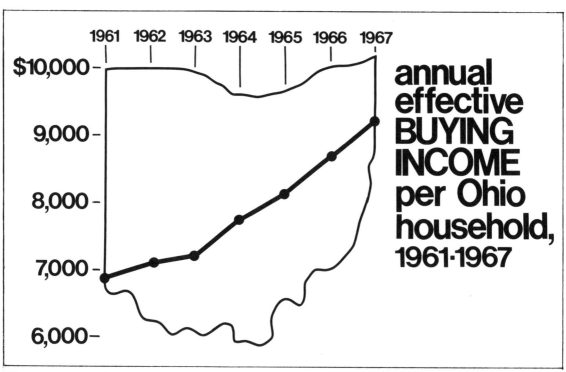

annual effective BUYING INCOME per Ohio household, 1961-1967

MAP/AREA GRAPH

Maps can serve as more than a conventional geographic reference; they offer a versatile and functional way of displaying numerical data. (See Figure 41.)

The map graph sometimes falls in the pictorial graph category. If thought of in this sense, the map can be employed as a backdrop for data or as an integral part of the data. In either case, whether local, state, national or international in nature, the presence of a map suggests to the viewer a geographical frame of reference as in Figure 42.

In Figure 43, the map is employed to orient the viewer to the data by states. The light to dark shading of the states indicates per capita income by state. The viewer can see area trends as well as each contiguous state's approximate per capita income.

The area graph, like the circle graph, divides the whole into its parts. Concrete or abstract shapes can be employed. In Figure 44, the area is divided up proportionally to indicate how the average dollar is spent.

Figure 43. A map graph

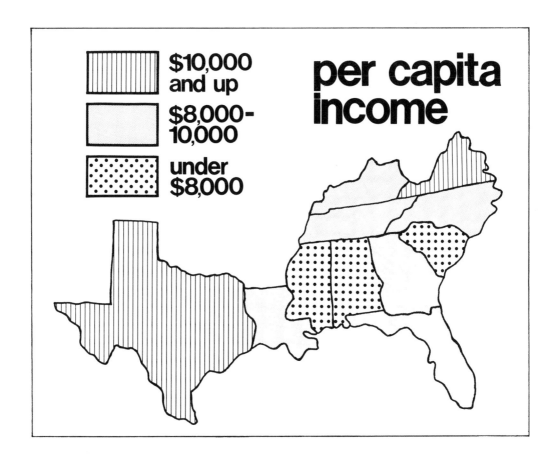

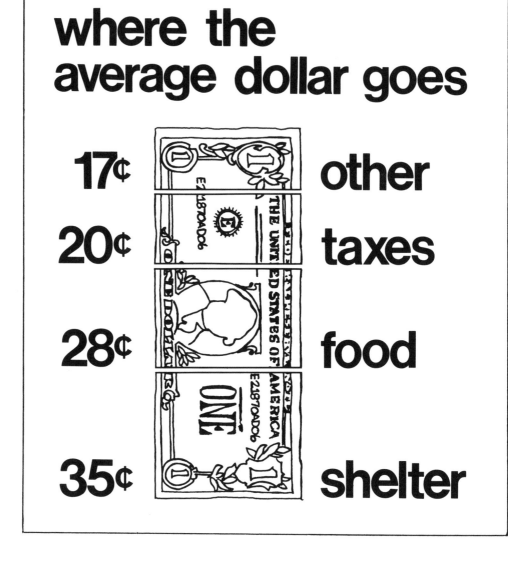

Figure 44.   Area graph dividing a whole into parts

The Titling of Graphs

Regardless of the format, most every graph carries with it a title or heading. There are basically two approaches to titling. One approach is to use the title to tell the audience the subject of the graph, "U.S. Birth Rate." The other approach is to tell the audience the major message or point of the graph, "U.S. Birth Rate Goes Down." Both approaches to titling have merit. Titles that emphasize the subject allow the viewer to come to a conclusion regarding the meaning of a graph. Titles that emphasize meaning help the audience see the significance of the data. For designers who like to have the major message in the title, perhaps a title such as "What's Happening to the U.S. Birth Rate?" is a good approach to directing attention to the message without directly telling the audience the message. Short, clear, unambiguous titles enhance the possibilities that viewers will get right to the visual aspect of the graph.

Many times, more than a title is necessary for efficient communication. Keys, secondary information and axis labels all require thoughtful planning. Again, clear, unambiguous language is your most effective approach. An over labeled graph is often confusing to the viewer.

Following, are four EXERCISES which contain data in tabular form. Each problem has many answers. You are encouraged to try to solve each problem by applying the various graphing formats discussed above. (Your first impulse might tell you that the data should be in a bar graph format. Do a rough thumbnail sketch using a bar graph. However, for additional sketches, explore, say, an area graph and a pictorial graph.)

After you have done some thumbnail sketches, look at the alternative solutions that appear at the end of this chapter. These alternatives combined with your alternatives should be proof that there is more than one way to communicate even the most elemental data.

EXERCISE IX

A Bit of Data

Dental Care for Children
Age 5–14   U.S. 1963–65

One child in every four had
never seen a dentist.

The above data are simple and straightforward. Rough sketch three alternative ways to present the above data as a graph. When your sketches are complete turn to Alternatives IXa, IXb, and IXc on pages 82–83.

EXERCISE X

Relationships of Data

Injuries resulting from accidents
(for children over 1 year of age)
USA 1966

Total Injuries	.19,000,000
1–17 years	
Home Injuries	.10,000,000
School Injuries	. 3,000,000
Street and Highway Injuries	. 2,000,000

The above data are fixed in time (1966) and cover total injuries resulting from accidents. There are several different points of emphasis that could be developed. Graph the above data at least three different ways. When your sketches are complete, turn to Alternatives Xa, Xb, Xc and Xd on pages 84–85.

EXERCISE XI

Progressions of Data

Hogs on Farms in the U.S.

1890	48,130,000	1940	61,165,000
1900	51,055,000	1950	58,937,000
1910	48,072,000	1960	59,026,000
1920	60,159,000	1970	57,046,000
1930	55,705,000		

The above data can be visualized to give the viewer a sense of the pig population trend. Rough sketch three approaches to graphing this data. Then, turn to Alternatives XIa, XIb and XIc on pages 86–87.

EXERCISE XII

A Relationship Between Progressions of Data

SCHOOL OF PUBLIC HEALTH
UNC-CHAPEL HILL

Students	447	468	480	545	573	512	520
Faculty	146	140	151	139	137	135	132
	1970–71	'71–'72	'72–'73	'73–'74	'74–'75	'75–'76	'76–'77

These data are at first glance rather simple and uncomplicated. As you sketch three ways to present the data remember that you are attempting to communicate something about the relationship that exists between these two progressions of data. Then, turn to Alternatives XIIa, XIIb and XIIc on pages 88–89.

The fact that there are circle graphs, line graphs, bar graphs, pictorial graphs, map and area graphs has been demonstrated. The major challenge comes in selecting the type of graph best suited to communicate data that has been generated in verbal or tabular form. This chapter should have given you a greater appreciation for the value of the graph. The EXERCISES should have stimulated your exploration of alternative graph formats.

EXERCISE IX

Dental Care for Children
Age 5–14   U.S. 1963–65

One child in every four had
never seen a dentist.

IXa.   This alternative emphasizes that the graph is about children. As you look at the sketch you can "see" that one out of every four children has never seen a dentist. Or, in a positive mode, you can "see" that three out of every four children have seen a dentist. Note that the title is a question that focuses on the major point raised by the data.

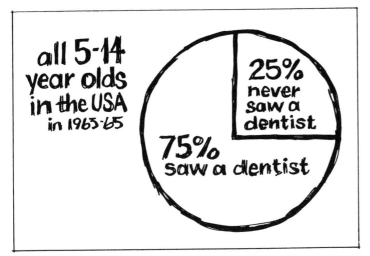

all 5-14 year olds in the USA in 1963-65

25% never saw a dentist

75% saw a dentist

IXb.   This alternative focuses on the total population of children and generalizes about them in terms of percentages. This use of a circle graph is easily "read" because a quarter of a circle is a very clear division of that shape. To further contribute to the meaning of the graph, illustrations or photographs could be incorporated within the circle graph. A child alone behind the 25% wedge and a child with a dentist behind the 75% wedge could aid the viewer in better understanding the message.

IXc.   This alternative is a variation on IXa and IXb. In this sketch, the viewer quickly sees where the data take place. There are four circles, each representing children. Circles are not as literal a graphic image as the silhouettes in IXa. However, the title helps the audience understand what each circle stands for.

one out of every four 5-14 yr. olds never saw a DENTIST (in 1963-65)

NO YES
YES YES

Injuries resulting from accidents
(for children over 1 year of age)
USA 1966

Total Injuries	. . . . . .	19,000,000
1–17 years		
Home Injuries	. . . .	10,000,000
School Injuries	. . . .	3,000,000
Street and Highway Injuries	.	2,000,000

Xa. This sketch emphasizes a comparison among the three major locations of accidents. The viewer is led to see that the home is the primary place where accidents occur.

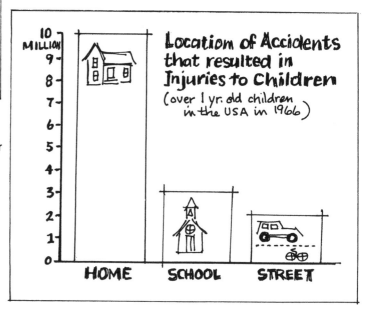

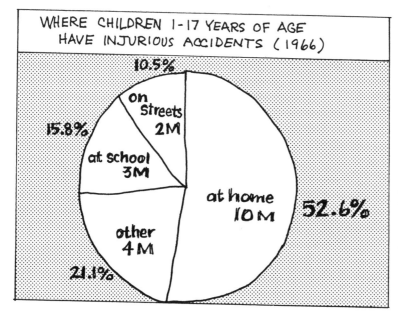

Xb. In this alternative, the emphasis is on the visualization of the total population. Note that another category—"other"—had to be included to complete this rendition.

Xc.   This example is a map of the child's world of home, street and school. Though this presentation does not give the viewer a feeling for volume, it does evoke a feeling of where these accidents took place.

Xd.   This alternative is a variation of Alternative Xa. Both representations emphasize that home is *the* place where the most accidents occur.
In this case, type size is the emphasizing device.

EXERCISE XI

Hogs on Farms in the U.S.			
1890	48,130,000	1940	61,165,000
1900	51,055,000	1950	58,937,000
1910	48,072,000	1960	59,026,000
1920	60,159,000	1970	57,046,000
1930	55,705,000		

All three sketches are built on the bar/line graph format. The primary difference among the ideas is the kind and quality of visual images used.

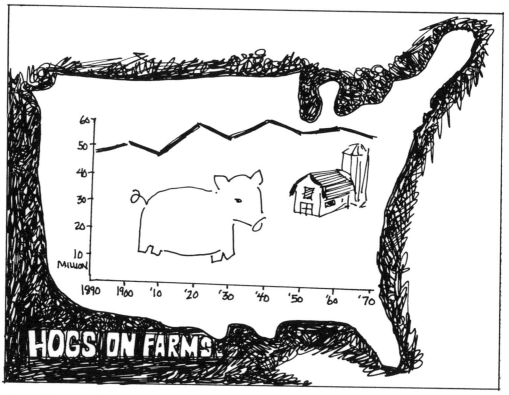

XIa.   This alternative tells the viewer *where* the data took place.

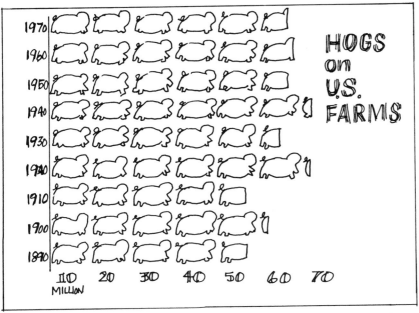

XIb. In this sketch pigs are used as place holders through time. Note that the vertical axis is used to depict time.

XIc. This is a conservative approach; it employs the vertical bar graph to demonstrate fluctuations in total population through the years.

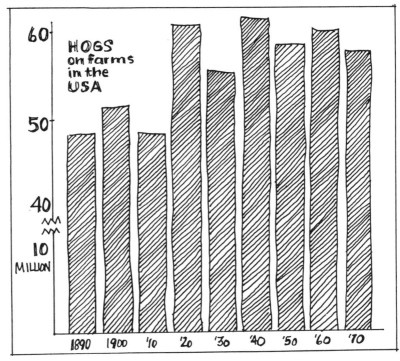

SCHOOL OF PUBLIC HEALTH
UNC-CHAPEL HILL

	1970–71	'71–'72	'72–'73	'73–'74	'74–'75	'75–'76	'76–'77
Students	447	468	480	545	573	512	520
Faculty	146	140	151	139	137	135	132

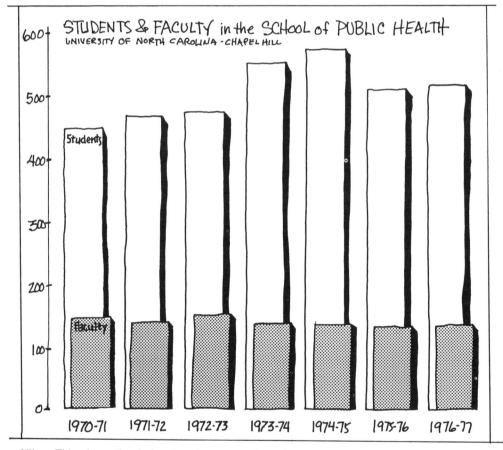

XIIa.   This alternative helps the viewer see the subtle rise and fall of the numbers of students and faculty in relation to each other. It emphasizes proportional relationships.

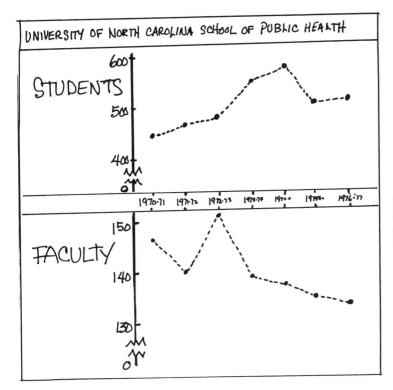

UNIVERSITY OF NORTH CAROLINA SCHOOL OF PUBLIC HEALTH

STUDENTS

600
500
400
0

1970-71 1971-72 1972-73 1973-74 1974-5 1975-6 1976-77

FACULTY

150
140
130
0

XIIb.   This sketch uses two different scales to help the viewer see the changes over time. It depicts a trend comparison.

XIIc.   This alternative uses a conversion of the enrollment data to faculty/student ratios.

SCHOOL OF PUBLIC HEALTH - UNIVERSITY OF NORTH CAROLINA · · · ·

FACULTY : STUDENT RATIO

1970-71	1 : 3.06
1971-72	1 : 3.43
1972-73	1 : 3.17
1973-74	1 : 3.96
1974-75	1 : 4.15
1975-76	1 : 3.80
1976-77	1 : 3.90

6 The Visualization of Broad Concepts

Often we teach broad concepts or large ideas. Some of these concepts are visible (a zoning plan for a community) and other concepts encompass that which is more or less invisible (a structuralist's theory of sociology). Regardless of how visible or invisible the concepts are, they demand our full talents in order to communicate them effectively. Both language and visualization are talents we can tap for assistance.

The larger the concept, the more complex the idea, the more abstract the theory, the more likely we will need to use some type of visualization to present these broad concepts. However, the presentation of theories and broad concepts is usually verbal. We *talk* about *ideas*. We *talk* because large ideas, by their very nature, usually have no obvious visual manifestation or counterpart. We visualize simple, concrete, well-known things, whereas, large concepts are usually presented verbally. It is with these broad ideas that we often have difficulty communicating. It seems reasonable to suggest that broad ideas need to be visualized as well as verbalized in order to give the learner at least two sets of stimuli as aids to understanding.

Teachers and others involved in communication are quick to give visual treatment to a subject if it lends itself to visualization. However, these same educators often shy from inventing new visual configurations to communicate subjects that do not lend themselves to quick visualization. Large ideas, by their very nature are difficult to conceptualize in visual form.

In this chapter we will attempt to communicate three kinds of visible broad concepts and three kinds of invisible concepts.

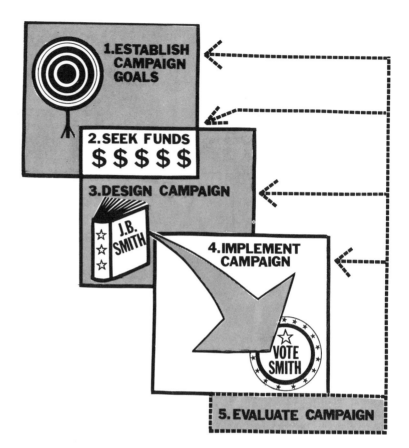

Figure 45.   Visualized plan

The three kinds of *visible concepts* are: Plans and Organizational charts, Maps and Chronologies.

The three kinds of *invisible concepts* are: Generalizations, Theories and Feelings and Attitudes.

Plans and Organizational Charts

Plans are sets of sequenced actions or goals. They are often presented as lists. For example, these are the five steps in a plan to run a campaign for office:

1. To establish goals
2. To seek funds and staff
3. To design the campaign
4. To implement the campaign
5. To evaluate the effect of the campaign

This plan can also be visualized. (Figure 45) The graphic images in each step of the plan help convey the meaning of each step. The visual layout of the words and images give clues to the interrelationship of each aspect of the plan.

THE GARDENER'S SCHEDULE FOR THE YEAR

Plan   Plant   Grow   Pick & Can   Rest

| jan | feb | mar | april | may | june | july | aug | sept | oct | nov | dec |

Figure 46. Visualization of relative time

Sometimes plans are tied closely to time. That is, we not only know what we will do, we know when and how long it will take to do it.

Figure 46 illustrates how to communicate graphically the function performed in each step of a plan and the relative time necessary to perform the function. The visual weight of the various steps gives the viewer a grasp of the amount of time to be spent.

Visualization can help clarify the various steps of a plan. Visualization can also aid in understanding the weight or significance of the various steps.

Organizational charts are visual displays of relationships among people in a given setting.

Lines and boxes are the cornerstone techniques used to communicate organizational charts. Figure 47 is a classic example of a line-and-staff organizational chart in which the viewer can quickly see line and staff relationships.

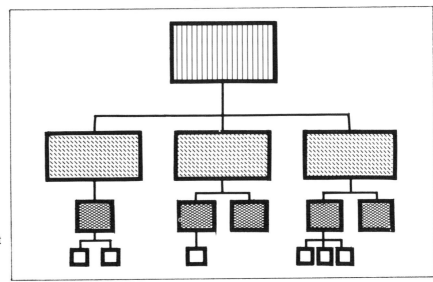

Figure 47. Line-and-staff organizational chart

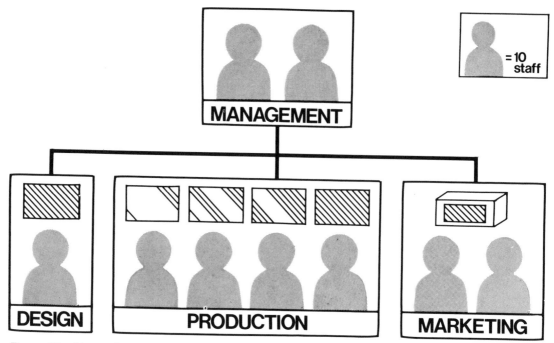

Figure 48. Line-and-staff *and* function relationships

Though the line-and-staff relationships are clear in Figure 47, the viewer is given no visual cues to meaning other than boxes and lines. Figure 48 is an attempt to give the viewer not only line-and-staff relationships but also visual cues to function.

EXERCISE XIII will give you an opportunity to visualize information about an organization.

EXERCISE XIII

The American Shovel Company has six divisions:

1. Administration
2. Design
3. Production
4. Advertising
5. Distribution
6. Sales

Visualize the functions and interrelationships of these functions. This display should be for a middle school learner. The learner should be able to list the six major divisions of consumer goods companies. Alternatives XIIIa, XIIIb and XIIIc on pages 106–107 are possible solutions.

MAPS

Maps are one of our oldest visual aids to learning. Scientists have given us a wealth of skills and techniques useful in accurate map making. This section will not deal with the science of maps but, rather, the art of maps as visual aids to learning.

What is the purpose of preparing a map? To illustrate the range and quality of a place? To give direction? To illustrate the relationship between demographic variables? To simulate the actual place? The purpose or function of the map will dictate the visualization.

3-D Maps

Three dimensional models have great visual appeal. Figure 49 is an example of a 3-D map. The use of symbols or models helps

Figure 49. 3-D map. (table top)

Figure 50. Floor map

to orient viewers to key elements or key landmarks. Three-dimensional maps can be experienced "live" as in table top models or relief maps, or may be seen as photographs of 3-D models.

Participation directly on a 3-D floor map is illustrated in Figure 50. Though no graphics or 3-D models are present in this example, they could be added to enhance a viewer's awareness of ideas. For example, 3-D models of major industrial products could be placed on the map in appropriate areas.

The Distorted Map

Usually a map is presented in such a way that the different areas of the map are in scale. That is, as you look at Figure 51 you can tell that Maine is the largest land area of the six New England States. However, sometimes we want to present a concept or idea that could distort the map. Figure 52 attempts to represent graphically the size of the population of each New England state. Note that Massachusetts is the largest state in terms of population in New England. Every attempt has been made, in Figure 52, to retain the overall general appearance of each state. Only the scale of relative size has been distorted.

Now complete EXERCISE XIV.

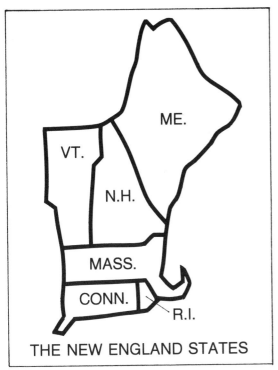

Figure 51.
Proportional
area map

THE NEW ENGLAND STATES

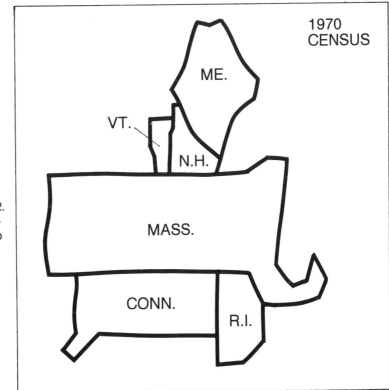

1970
CENSUS

Figure 52.
Distorted·
area map

EXERCISE XIV

You want to communicate the three major geographic regions of North Carolina:

1. Coastal Plains (elevation range 0 to 300 feet) east
2. Piedmont (elevation range 300 to 1,500) central
3. Mountains (elevation range 1,500 to 6,000) west

The following map can be used as a reference:

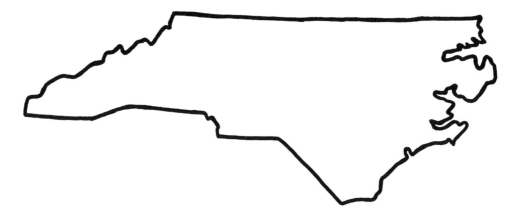

Rough sketch a design for a slide to help communicate this information.

Alternatives XIVa, XIVb, XIVc on page 108 are possible solutions.

Chronologies

When dealing with major historic events, periods or concepts, it is often a challenge to keep time in proper perspective. For example, oil is a finite natural resource that was formed over millions of years and we are consuming it in hundreds of years. There are time-related problems that contribute to our understanding of this relationship. Figure 53 is a time line that visualizes the time necessary to accomplish each portion of the bread baking process.

Often we want to communicate the historic evolution of a concept or idea. The time line is a classic example. Figure 54 illustrates the evolution of ship design. Note that the viewer can see the relative active and inactive periods of invention. Turn to EXERCISE XV.

Figure 53. Proportional time line

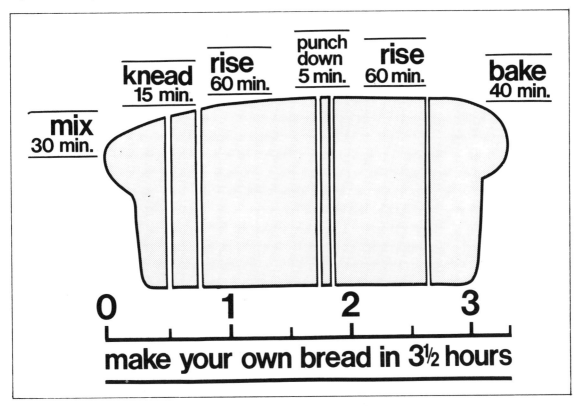

1850
1800

1450
1300

500 A.D.

2,000 B.C.

The
Development
of the Ship

3,000 B.C.

Figure 54.   Historic time line

EXERCISE XV

You are to communicate the evolution of five major painting schools. (All dates are approximate.)

1. Neo-classicism—(1830–1860)
2. Impressionism—(1875–1910)
3. Cubism—(1900–1920)
4. Abstract expressionism—(1920–1960)
5. Pop art—(1960–1970)

Rough sketch a design for a wall poster to help communicate the above information. (You may need to do some research on each school.) Alternatives XVa, XVb and XVc on page 109 are possible solutions.

Invisible Concepts

That which is invisible is the most difficult to communicate. Yet oddly enough, these invisible concepts are in most need of help in order to be understood. We explain, then, one way and then another. Explaining can take us through our complete repertoire of verbal skills. We describe, we compare, we establish analogies, we invent mnemonic devices, (e.g. "A Cow Eats Grass," "Every Good Boy Does Fine"), we give examples. Regardless of our technique, we give the concept a good "verbal going over." Since our audience usually has eyes as well as ears, perhaps a visualization of the concept may increase the possibility that they may understand the message.

Attempts to visualize the invisible will more than likely result in new constructs or new ways to conceive ideas. But just as we have a variety of ways to describe, we have a variety of ways to depict visually. The exploration of these variations has been traversed for visible ideas; now the challenge is to work on invisible ideas.

We will look at three types of invisible concepts:
1. Generalizations
2. Theories
3. Feelings and Attitudes

GENERALIZATIONS

Every discipline or field of inquiry evolves a series of generalizations. Usually these are the result of a great deal of synthesizing behavior by scholars in that field or discipline. Sometimes we want the learner to develop his or her own generalizations, and this is a reasonable expectation. But more often than not we want to communicate a generalization to the learner. For example, we would like the learner to know the following generalization:

Nomadic, agricultural and technological societies have different relationships with the environment. We describe concrete examples that lead to this generalization. Examples such as:

Nomads drink from ponds, farmers dig watering holes, and technologists dam and process water. (see Figure 55) Or, nomads pick and eat what grows naturally, agrarians plant crops to eat, technologists grow food in "non-soil" in greenhouses.

EXERCISE XVI will give you an opportunity to visualize a generalization.

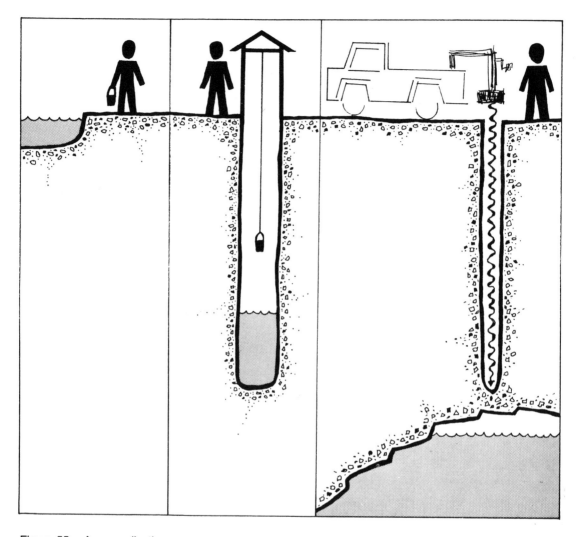

Figure 55.　A generalization

EXERCISE XVI

Design a visual display that helps junior high school learners understand the following generalization: *the investment potential of a nation is primarily influenced and governed by how much money each citizen of that nation saves in a licensed bank in that nation.*

Alternatives XVIa, XVIb and XVIc on pages 110–111 are possible solutions.

THEORIES

Theories are verified or conjectured formulations about underlying artistic or scientific principles. Einstein's theory of relativity is a classic example. Theories abound in all fields. Often these theories are complex, abstract or "pure." Given these characteristics, it is no small wonder that many theories are difficult to comprehend and, further, to visualize. Again, we use words to explain meaning and neglect the visual aspect. A judicious combination of words and images could add significantly to the understanding of most theories.

Figure 56 is an attempt to visualize the Shannon-Weaver model of communication.

Theories, models, abstractions and the like are challenging to visualize because they often demand invention of new visual configurations. Turn to EXERCISE XVII.

Figure 56.   A theory (communication model)

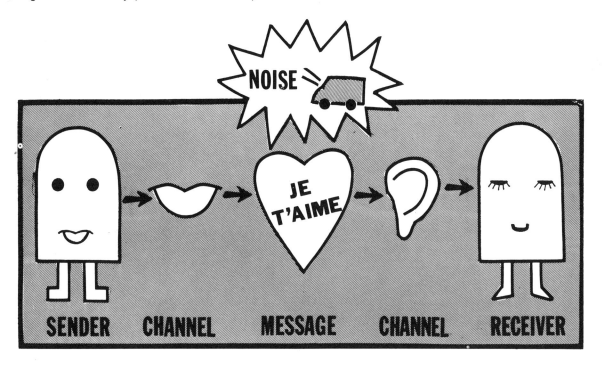

FEELINGS AND ATTITUDES

Sometimes we want to communicate pure feelings such as joy or the concept of willing cooperation or the sense of loneliness. At other times, we want to communicate processes, data, theories and the like, in a way that they also include feelings or attitudes. For example, it is easier to communicate how to brush your teeth than it is to create the desire to brush your teeth.

We can obviously take photographs with or about feelings and we can write with or about feelings. Likewise, we can develop graphic symbols that evoke feelings. Figure 57 is an example of a "reader slide" that attempts to elicit feelings. Rusty barbed wire should bring forth strong feelings; the emotional connotation of barbed wire is stronger than the "turned away" or "unfriendly" conventional descriptors for alienation.

Now try the following EXERCISE.

Figure 57. Visualization of feelings incorporated in a "reader slide"

The purpose of visualizing broad concepts is to increase the possibilities that our educational messages are understood. Clearly, if the visualization is poorly conceived it is possible that it could obstruct communication.

Visualization can be a new way to look at things we normally see and take for granted. Visualization may be a new way to conceptualize an idea that heretofore had only been talked about.

The American Shovel Company has six divisions:
1. Administration
2. Design
3. Production
4. Advertising
5. Distribution
6. Sales

EXERCISE XIII

XIIIa. Concept related graphics visually supporting company shovel.

XIIb. Visualizes the idea of all functions taking place in one building.

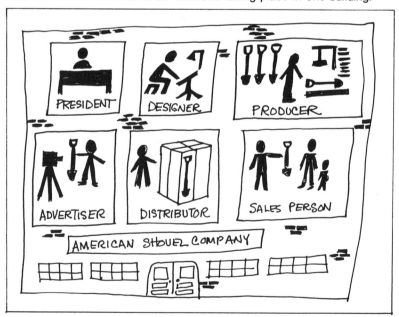

XIIIc. Shows linear relationship of the functions.

1. Coastal Plains (elevation range 0 to 300 feet) east
2. Piedmont (elevation range 300 to 1,500) central
3. Mountains (elevation range 1,500 to 6,000) west

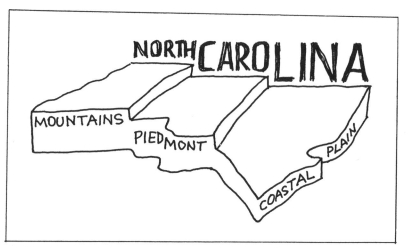

XIVa.   The differences in elevations are stressed.

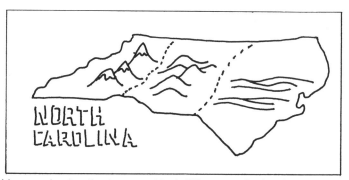

XIVb.   Graphics emphasize the topographical differences in the three areas.

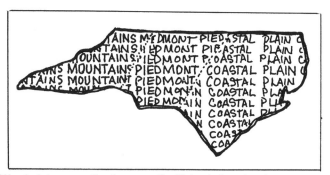

XIVc.   Words take on a "wallpaper effect" to define the three areas.

Major Painting Schools

1. Neo-classicism—(1830–1860)
2. Impressionism—(1875–1910)
3. Cubism—(1900–1920)
4. Abstract expressionism—(1920–1960)
5. Pop art—(1960–1970)

EXERCISE XV

XVa. The paintings are proportional vertically as well as horizontally.

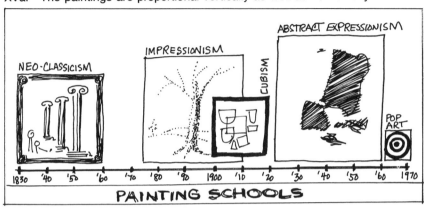

XVb. The same subject rendered by artists of the five schools.

XVc. A comparison of the length of each school.

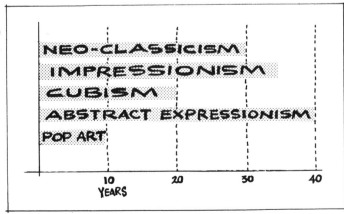

EXERCISE XVI

the investment potential of a nation
is primarily influenced and governed
by how much money each citizen
of that nation saves in a licensed
bank in that nation.

XVIa.   Arrows help direct the viewer's attention.

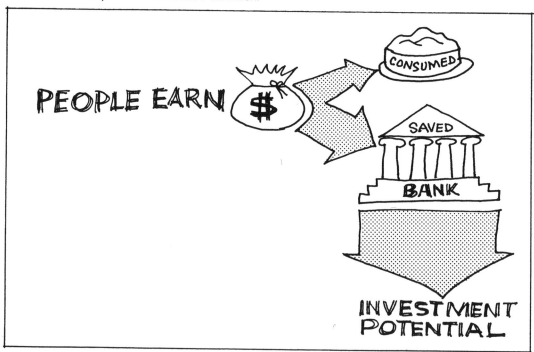

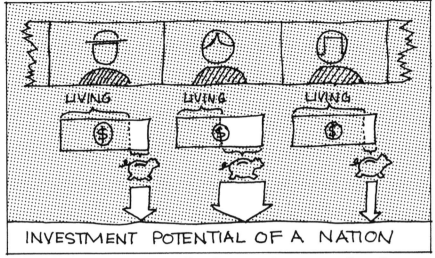

INVESTMENT POTENTIAL OF A NATION

XVIb.   Some people save more than others.

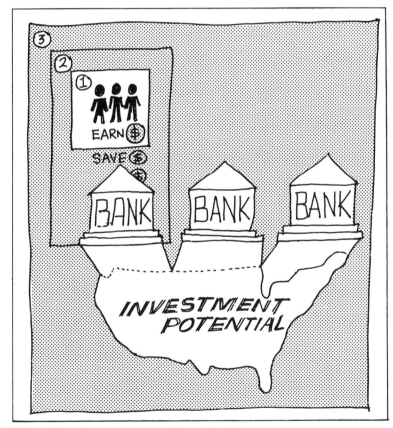

XVIc.   Use of screens serves to emphasize.

EXERCISE XVII

the more things change
the more they remain the same.

XVIIa. "Split screen" effect emphasizes the meaning of the generalization.

XVIIb. The learner should remain "the same."

XVIIc. The globes should look exactly alike in design.

EXERCISE XVIII

cooperation exists among

principal
teacher
student

PRINCIPAL   TEACHER   LEARNER

XVIIIa.   Holding hands is a
"cooperating" image.

XVIIIb.   Pillars support
"cooperate" to
"hold up" the school.

XVIIIc.   The triangle and overlapping images
contribute to "cooperative feelings."

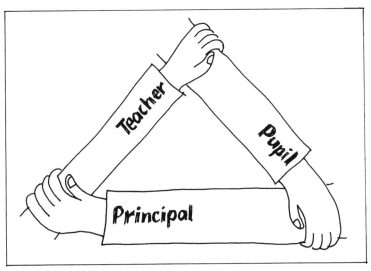

7 Field Testing and Rendering

Visual thinking, conceptualizing, designing and communicating have been the major foci of this book. Your skills have been tested as you sought alternative approaches to the various EXERCISES. You have been challenged to think in visual terms and to rough sketch visual ideas. Often you entertained more than one visual idea or conceptualization. Which one of your many ideas is the best one? Which is the most instructional? Which is the most efficient and effective? Which is the most attention getting? Which is the most asthetically pleasing? And once this "best" one has been chosen, how should you convert the thumbnail sketch into finished art? This chapter will focus on field testing and rendering considerations that will help answer these questions.

Choosing Your Best Alternative

Two good ideas may be worse than one good idea. That is, it might prove to be quite a dilemma, trying to decide which of two or more good ideas is the one that will communicate the message.

Often you can tell from your own experiences which of your ideas or rough sketches is best. Perhaps an even better way to decide among alternatives is to field test your ideas on their intended audience. Who is the display for? This intended audience (e.g. third graders or first year nursing students) will be very helpful in selecting appropriate visual aids.

Select a small sample (six might do) of your intended audience. Arrange to talk to them privately; as you begin your interview tell the interviewee the purpose or goal of the visual presentation. (i.e., "The visual aids I will show you are intended to help you name the four phases of the combustion engine"). Next, show your interviewee your alternate sketches. Ask him or her to rank the sketches in order of preference. If possible ask that he or she tell you why the alternatives are ranked in that particular order.

This preference testing by a sample of your audience can help you decide which alternative to have rendered into final form. However, the fact that the intended audience *preferred* one sketch over another may not necessarily mean that the preferred sketch will produce the most learning.

You can, of course, field test the sketches regarding learning gain. This technique requires some advance planning. The intended audience sample (in this case 18) must be identified. Give the sample a pre-test on the information in the display. Show each alternative to a subgroup of the sample. For example show Alternative A to the first six people in the sample, show Alternative B to the second six people in the sample, show Alternative C to the third six people in the sample. Next, give a post-test. The alternative that produces significant learning gain may well be your best example; however, that which is significant may be difficult to discern without using statistical methods.

Sophisticated field testing of alternative ideas through audience preference testing and/or assessing learning gain is time consuming. Often, you do not have the time nor the resources for such sophisticated research. If you do choose the route of developing a meaningful field test, a word of caution. Be sure that your institution (or client) is committed to giving time to evaluating and using the results to advantage. And, too, if you plan ample time for field testing, do it in a highly professional manner.

Rendering Your Visual Presentations

Once a thumbnail sketch has been selected to use, the next task is to render it in a final form. Is it to be a slide, an overhead transparency, a two-dimensional display, a board game or some other medium? Format cost restrictions and design considerations will influence the way you choose to render the finished product. Kemp, Wright, Minor and Frye, give you helpful information regarding these aspects.

Who will actually do the rendering? You can do it or you can get someone else to render your idea.

If you render the finished product, work from your strengths. That is, if you work well in pen and ink, render your idea in pen and ink techniques. Don't try to work in materials or techniques that are the materials and techniques of someone else! Don't imitate others! Be yourself. The results of your work will have much more integrity and personality than if you were to imitate someone else. You may find that you render ideas in one medium better than another. That is, you may render art for slides much better than you render art for overhead transparences. If so, you've found a strength—work from it.

This is not to say that you should not work on your weaknesses. You should be working to add to your repertoire of skills. You should recognize your strengths, and use them. You should not be preoccupied with your weaknesses and attempts to become something you are not.

If you are going to ask someone else to render art work for you, here are some suggestions. Ask to see the artist's portfolio. An artist that works well in one medium does not necessarily work well in another medium. For instance, if you are in need of completing a 3-D display, look for an artist/designer who has had display design experience.

Give the artist specific and clear directions. Your thumbnail sketch may need to be clarified. Specify color, layout, type size and style, rendering medium and the like. Be sure your artist understands the directions. Do not be ambiguous or vague. Clear directions can lead to a usable product. Vague directions can lead to well designed products that are not usable. Time is usually a major factor. Your artist will have to work under some time restriction.

Artists who render desirable aids for learning must be willing to take direction from the educational message designer. That is, a visual display may well embody good graphic design qualities but not contribute to the learning of the audience. Clearly both the conceptualizer and the renderer must be willing to return to the drawing board to re-think and re-do the visual plan and/or the visual product. Visual thinking, therefore, is a process that requires exercising your skills and expanding your repertoire. Educational message designers and message renderers must work together to generate original, well conceived visualizations that can improve as well as inspire learning.

Bibliography

Books

Albers, Josef. *Interaction of Color.* New Haven, Connecticut: Yale University Press, 1963, 80 pp.

Anderson, Ronald H. *Selecting and Developing Media for Instruction.* New York: Van Nostrand Reinhold Company, 1976, 138 pp.

Archigraphia. Edited by Walter Herdeg. New York: Hastings House, 1978, 236 pp.

Clarke, Beverley. *Graphic Design in Educational Television.* New York: Watson-Guptill Publications, 1974, 96 pp.

Creativity in Communication. Edited by Robert Adams. Greenwich, Connecticut, New York Graphic Society Limited, 1971, 151 pp.

de Sausmarez, Maurice. *Basic Design: The Dynamics of Visual Form.* New York: Reinhold Publishing Corporation, 1964, 96 pp.

Diethelm, Walter. *Form and Communication.* Zurich, ABC Editions, 1974, 227 pp.

Dondas, Donis A. *Primer of Visual Literacy.* Cambridge, Massachusetts: MIT Press, 1974, 194 pp.

Dreyfuss, Henry. *Symbol Sourcebook.* New York: McGraw-Hill Book Company, 1972, 292 pp.

Education of Vision. Edited by Gyorgy Kepes. New York: George Braziller, 1965, 233 pp.

Film and TV Graphics. Edited by Walter Herdeg. Zurich: The Graphic Press, 1967, 199 pp.

Fletcher, Alan et al. *Graphic Design: Visual Comparisons.* New York: Reinhold Publishing Corporation, 1964, 94 pp.

Graphis Diagrams. Edited by Walter Herdeg. Zurich: The Graphis Press. Distributed by Hastings House, 1974, 183 pp.

Gray, Bill. *Studio Tips for Artists and Graphic Designers.* New York: Van Nostrand Reinhold Company, 1976, 128 pp.

Halas, John. *Visual Scripting.* New York: Hastings House, 1976, 144 pp.

Hilliard, Robert L. *Writing for Television and Radio.* New York: Hastings House, 1976, 320 pp.

Hurrell, Ron. *Manual of Television Graphics.* New York: Van Nostrand Reinhold Company, 1973, 136 pp.

Kemp, Gerald. *Planning and Producing Audiovisual Materials.* Third edition, New York: Thomas Y. Crowell Company, 1975, 320 pp.

Kepes, Gyorgy. *Language of Vision.* Chicago, Illinois: Paul Theobald, 1964, 228 pp.

Kinsey, Anthony. *How to Make Animated Movies.* New York: The Viking Press, 1970, 95 pp.

Koch, Rudolf. *The Book of Signs.* New York: Dover Publications, 1930, 104 pp.

Laughton, Roy. *TV Graphics.* New York: Reinhold Publishing Corporation, 1966, 94 pp.

Lewis, John. *Typography: Basic Principles, Influences and Trends Since the Nineteenth Century.* New York: Reinhold Publishing Corporation, 1964, 96 pp.

McKim, Robert H. *Experiences in Visual Thinking.* Monterey, California: Brooks/Cole Publishing Company, 1972, 171 pp.

Minor, Ed & Harvey R. Frye. *Techniques for Producing Visual Instructional Media.* New York: McGraw-Hill Book Company, 1970, 305 pp.

Nelms, Henning. *Thinking with a Pencil.* New York: Barnes & Noble Incorporated, 1964, 347 pp.

Ogg, Oscar. *The 26 Letters.* New York: The Thomas Y. Crowell Company, 1961, 262 pp.

Pye, David. *The Nature of Design.* New York: Reinhold Publishing Corporation, 1964, 96 pp.

Research, Principles and Practices in Visual Communication. Edited by John Ball and Francis Byrnes. Washington, D.C.: Association for Educational Communications and Technology, 1960, 160 pp.

Samuels, Mike and Nancy Samuels. *Seeing with the Minds Eye.* New York: Random House · Bookworks Book, 1975, 331 pp.

Satterthwaite, Les. *Graphics: Skills, Media and Materials.* Third edition, Dubuque, Iowa: Kendall/Hunt Publishing Company, 1977, 218 pp.

Saul, Ezra, & others (prepared). *A Review of the Literature Pertinent to the Design and Use of Effective Graphic Training Aids.* Technical Report, SDC 494–08–1. Port Washington, Long Island, New York: U.S. Naval Training Device Center, 1954, 216 pp.

Stankowski, Anton. *Visual Presentation of Invisible Processes.* Switzerland: Arthur Niggli Limited, 1966, 127 pp.

Wright, Andrew. *Designing for Visual Aids.* New York: Van Nostrand Reinhold Company, 1970, 96 pp.

Annuals

1. *Art Directors Annual:* New York Art Directors Club, Edited by Kevin McCoy. New York: Watson-Guptill.
2. *Graphis Annual.* Edited by Walter Herdeg. Zurich, Switzerland: distributed in United States by Hastings House Publishers, New York.
3. *Penrose Graphic Arts International Annual.* Edited by Bryan Smith, London, England: distributed in United States by Hastings House Publishers, New York.

1. *Communication Arts.* Coyne & Blanchard Incorporated, Palo Alto, California.
2. *Graphis.* International Journal for Graphic and Applied Art. Zurich, Graphis Press, distributed in the United States by Hastings House Publishers, New York.
3. *Print.* R. C. Publications, New York.
4. *U & LC* (upper and lower case). International Typeface Corporation, New York.

Index